an overachiever's guide to breaking the rules

how to let go of perfect and live your truth

heather whelpley

MINNEAPOLIS

ISBN 13: 978-1-63489-460-9
LCCN: 2020913606

Printed in the United States of America
First Printing: 2021

25 24 23 22 21 5 4 3 2 1

Cover design by Zoe Norvell
Interior design by Patrick Maloney

Wise Ink Creative Publishing
807 Broadway St NE
Suite 46
Minneapolis, MN, 55413

contents

introduction

A few years ago, my parents moved out of my childhood home to a smaller house down the road. This meant I *finally* had to sort through things that never made it out of my teenage bedroom and into my adult home. I was thirty-six; it was time.

The closet was sparse and easy to clean out. The massive Spanish-English dictionary I'd bought for AP Spanish my senior year in high school, which had probably been obsolete seventeen of the eighteen years I'd owned it, was easily tossed into the recycle pile. The contents of the bulletin board that hung on my wall for years were slipped into a folder for safekeeping. My mom decided to keep my Cabbage Patch dolls, the prized possessions of my early elementary years, along with the clothes my great-aunt Emma had made for them. The remaining stuffed animals, random books, and photos were all easily sorted.

Then I embarked on my desk. Despite clearing nearly everything else out of my room years earlier, my desk was still full to the brim with journals, poems, and stories I'd written from ages eight to eighteen. Instead of shoving it all into a box and calling it a day, I pulled out a stack of poems and settled in for a journey through my teen years.

There was no shortage of emotional drama contained inside my desk. The boys I obsessed over who never even knew I was interested. An entire poem written about the time Rayanne betrayed Angela in *My So-Called Life* (yes, I wrote a poem about fictional characters in a TV show). Slightly more interesting poems about my hopes and dreams and changing the world.

And then I found this:

In just a few days my new life will start
A life of fun, freedom, and newness
A life of which I know not one part
The possibilities are endless they say
For this new life of excitement
But also chances to fall along the way
Failing is not a possibility for me
I've always walked, run, jumped, and skipped
That's how I must always be
But what if I do fall?
What will everyone say?
My parents, my teachers, all the people,
Who helped me along the way.
Will they still be proud to announce my name?
To them, will I always be the same?
What would I be without the trophies,
The achievements, the honors, the plaques?
Would I still be me?

Tears were streaming down my face by the time I finished reading the poem. I had no recollection of writing it. There was no date written on the loose-leaf paper, but I must have written it in the summer between high school graduation and starting college.

I felt the weight of my eighteen-year-old self. My soul

ached for her, this girl who felt like she wasn't allowed to fail before she'd even started living. The person afraid she would let everyone down if she were anything less than perfect. The young woman who attached her entire identity to achievements that really didn't matter much in the real world.

I have been the classic overachiever since birth. I was the valedictorian of my high school class, president of our school's chapter of the National Honor Society, and captain of two sports. I worked at my church, headed up the blood drive, participated in plays, volunteered, and babysat. No one made me do it. I was *driven*.

I knew I was smart, but I didn't feel like I was the smartest kid in my grade. I worked my tail off for every A I got. Friends who studied half as much as I did got grades that were almost as good. I got a 5 (the highest grade) on the AP US History test my sophomore year in high school because I reread *the entire textbook* in the month preceding the exam. Every day, I came home from school, exercised, and then studied for hours. When the little piece of paper came in the mail saying I'd gotten a 5, it all felt worth it.

I was exhausted all the time. In the winter of my junior year, I had cross-country ski practice every Saturday morning. We were all expected to be there, but, as captain, I really didn't have an option. I also worked at my church every Sunday starting at seven in the morning. This meant I didn't have a single day to sleep in for weeks. You can imagine how this felt to a teenager.

There was one beautiful Saturday on the horizon with nothing scheduled. I can't explain how much I was looking forward to sleeping in that day. Over twenty years later I can still feel the desperation and yearning I felt to just *sleep*.

A few weeks before the appointed day, I got a letter saying I'd been selected to interview for a mentoring program for my senior year of high school. The interview time? Eight in the morning on the one Saturday I had off.

I crumbled to the kitchen floor, curled up under the island, and sobbed. I'd put all my hope into this one morning and now it was gone.

My mom found me a few minutes later. "What's wrong?" she asked, alarmed.

"This was my one day to sleep in," I managed to get out between sobs, "and now I have to interview."

My mom took one look at me and without a moment's hesitation said, "You have to quit working at church."

I loved working at church, but I didn't put up any fight. A big part of me was relieved that someone else made the decision for me. I didn't know how to set my own boundaries, but at seventeen, my mom could do it for me.

Unfortunately, I didn't learn my lesson that day. I continued to push to—and often past—my breaking point. I almost blacked out during one of my finals in college because of the pressure I put on myself to get into a competitive study abroad program in Costa Rica. I got shingles when I was just thirty while burning the candle at both ends during a big project at work. I didn't take a single day off. No one suggested that I should, and my mom wasn't there to set the boundaries like she did when I was in high school.

Life wasn't drudgery—not by any stretch of the imagination. I had a *lot* of fun. I traipsed around the world my first few years after college, teaching environmental education in New England and leading trips with teens in the United States and Latin America. That didn't change after moving into a corporate job. I always made time for friends and fun.

Even within the fun, I pushed hard and acted like the overachieving valedictorian I was. By the end of my first season of teaching environmental education, I would fall asleep within five minutes of sitting anywhere. It turns out you can't teach fourteen hours a day, go to a bar at night, and party on the weekend without there being some consequences. Who knew?

I overdid *everything*. I ate too much, exercised even when my legs were screaming at me, checked email at eleven at night, and refused to compromise my social life. The overachiever in me wanted everything bigger, better, and now.

I often got it. I worked like crazy, but I was usually successful the first time I did something new. People noticed, especially after I started working in the corporate world. They told me I had "potential." Leaders treated me like an equal, despite the fact that I was many years and pay grades below them. I was selected to spend a year working in Australia.

For the most part, my outer world was working. My inner world was a little iffier. I felt the same weight I had at eighteen when I wrote the poem. *What would I be without the trophies, the achievements, the honors, the plaques? Would I still be me?*

My whole life has been a pull between the voice of the overachieving perfectionist and my true inner voice—the voice that wants to excel and make an impact, but in a healthy way. My true inner voice is creative and free-spirited and outspoken and calm. My true inner voice knows exactly who I am and doesn't require a single trophy, honor, or plaque for validation.

Slowly but surely, I've worked to free myself from hustling. I've let go of tying my worth to achievement. I've released myself from whatever grading system I happened to be a part of at the time, from report cards to performance reviews to my number of followers on Instagram. Most important, I've learned to trust my true inner voice and follow my authentic path.

It has taken me years and I still have to watch for the red flags that I'm paying more attention to the inner critic valedictorian than my true inner voice. Every year the cycle gets shorter and I return to myself faster. Every year I slow down a little more. Every year I cut another piece of the thread tying my worth to achievement. Every year my true voice gets a little louder and a little more public. Every year I'm a little more me.

This book is partially a memoir of my journey to letting go of the overachiever and reconnecting to my true self. I'll be sharing my stories and stories from my clients throughout the book, but it is written for you. At its heart, this book is about letting go of the rules you've been taught so you can create your own rules for life on your terms. My hope is that you'll release driving for perfection and unhealthy achieving so that you can return to yourself, follow your authentic path, and boldly use your true voice in the world to make a difference.

Several chapters have reflections and exercises to apply

directly to your life. Do them! You'll get so much more value from this book if you take the time to do the exercises. There is no magic in reading a book—the magic is in doing the work.

The book is broken into two parts:

- *How did you get here?* This section digs into all the reasons you got into manic achieving mode in the first place. We'll dive deep into what you're proving with over-achieving, the stories and lies of the inner critic, imposter syndrome, and the rules you're following, so you can change your story and let go of those rules. Do not skip this section! It may be the less "fun" part of the book, but it's the most important. Without understanding why and how you're operating now, you can't make lasting change.

- *Reconnect with yourself.* Section two is all about getting back to you. Reclaiming your true self—the person you are at the core. The person who is buried beneath layers of expectations and to-do lists and pressure to succeed. She's still in there, I promise. This section will show you step by step how to get back in touch with her through reawakening your true inner voice, restoring quiet in your life, reconnecting to your body, reclaiming joy, and rediscovering your creativity (no skill or artistry required!). You'll redefine success based on the desires of your true self, the woman you've reconnected with. Finally, you'll reset boundaries needed to keep you connected to yourself and learn to reform the fear and discomfort that surfaces when you slow down to take a breath.

There is also one final chapter on continuing the journey. It's about recognizing the red flags of overachiever mode and living your true voice to make an impact in the world. This book isn't a one and done. It's a way of living and being. It's something you'll come back to again and again, in the same way you will come back to yourself again and again.

The number one regret of the dying is wishing they'd had the courage to live a life true to themselves, not the life others expected of them. Yes, this might sound a bit dramatic, but it's the truth. This doesn't need to be your regret. Take this opportunity. Do the exercises in the book. Let go of the burden of expectations. Reconnect to yourself. Live the life of your true voice.

PART ONE

how did you get here?

CHAPTER ONE

what are you proving?

Looking back, there were several "red flag" moments where I could have stepped back and reflected on why I felt the constant need to achieve. Maybe I was a little young during the complete-exhaustion-sobbing-on-the-kitchen-floor incident in high school, but there were plenty of other warnings. For example, there was the time I started crying in a meeting with someone I barely knew while we were discussing a job opportunity for me. I was so overwhelmed with the amount of work on my plate for my current job that I couldn't even think about the future. There were also the semiannual upper respiratory infections that always arose when I took on too much, both at work and in my personal life. I definitely wasn't paying attention to the millions of times I said yes to yet another task when I really should have said no.

It wasn't until last winter that I finally understood why I had experienced red flag after red flag without making any changes in my life. I was one year into my business and working to launch a group coaching program for women experiencing imposter syndrome. I had piloted the program with a small group in the fall, and it was amazing. I loved it and the participants loved it. I saw them understand that the inner critic didn't need to have control over their lives. They realized their own strength and started to take a stand for what they wanted (and didn't want!) in their careers. It was unbelievably inspiring to see them evolve. I was convinced this was going to be *the* thing to make my business successful—and make a difference for women.

In November, I hired Allie, a digital marketer, for $5,000—the most I had spent on anything in my business by a long shot. At that point, I was putting enough pressure on myself already, and the money just added another layer. On top of that, I felt like I had to get everything ready to launch by January 1 to catch the New Year fever for self-improvement. I also decided to sell the condo I had lived in for ten years during this same time period. Because I clearly didn't have enough to do already.

Together, Allie and I worked to set up freebies and ads and webinars—all the things needed to attract new people to this coaching program. I put my head down and didn't look up from my work. I sat on my couch at night designing sales pages while Hallmark Christmas movies played in the background. I woke up in the morning thinking about Facebook ads.

I got it all done. I didn't enjoy my life much, and I had a complete breakdown on December 21, when I cried during my entire hour-long phone call with Allie, but I got it done. I launched January 2 to a complete and total deafening silence.

The entire thing failed. No one signed up for my coaching program.

Still determined to succeed and get my money's worth out of working with Allie, I quickly pivoted and launched a different coaching program for new women entrepreneurs dealing with doubt and imposter syndrome. This meant more freebies and Facebook ads and sales pages. I hosted a five-day challenge to launch the program. I hustled and hustled and kept right on hustling.

The second program failed too.

I was devastated. I had never failed this big *once* in my life, let alone twice in the span of three months. I felt like I wasted money (not just the $5,000 working with Allie, but another $2,000 on Facebook ads) and time and energy on something that gave me *zero* results, aside from some new Instagram followers and a few hundred people on my email list.

Even more than that, I hadn't enjoyed life for the last three months. I hated the way it felt to be driven all the time. I was always thinking about the launches. I constantly checked clicks and conversions on Facebook ads and worried when they were below what they were "supposed" to be. I compared myself to friends and strangers who looked like they had über-successful businesses and wondered what I was doing wrong.

I was getting plenty of sleep, but I was mentally, emotionally, and spiritually exhausted. I didn't want to keep living this way.

Unlike past red flags when I had pushed through these feelings and kept moving toward the next thing, this time I stopped. I asked myself *why* I was driving and pushing and feeling like everything had to be successful right out of the gate.

The answer came to me in an instant.

I was working so hard to prove myself. To compensate

for the areas in my life where I felt behind or out of the race entirely.

And the roots went back. *Way* back.

It started in seventh grade when I gained thirty pounds in my first semester of middle school. Although I was never a small child, I went from being an average weight to flat-out overweight in less than five months. No one teased me about my weight, thankfully, but I looked around at my school filled with pretty size 2 girls and knew I wasn't one of them. I saw the awkward flirtation between girls and boys, but I wasn't taking part in it. I had many friends who were boys, but there was a whole world that felt separate to me. No matter how hard I worked, I couldn't be part of that world.

School, on the other hand, was an area where I knew I could succeed. I could outwork anyone. The overachiever in me really took off at the end of ninth grade when I realized I was ranked number one in my class. I pushed every day for the next three years to stay there.

It wasn't just academics—it was church and sports and volunteering and leadership. I pushed myself to excel in every area where I had control. I worked every day to be perfect to make up for my weight. I drove myself into the ground to compensate for boys never being interested in me.

And I had no idea I was doing it.

Fast-forward to my twenties. I spent a few years traipsing the globe and following my free-spirited true inner voice after college. I lost fifty pounds. I started my corporate job. I did major work to appreciate my body, but I was still single.

And I was still driving to compensate for every place I felt behind in my life.

I turned thirty-nine during the failed launches of my coaching programs. I was single and didn't have any children, two things I never thought I'd be at thirty-nine, but I had my business.

I felt like my business *had* to be successful, because if I failed there and I wasn't married and wasn't a mother, then what did I have to show for my life?

On the other hand, if I had a successful business and made a huge impact, then it would be okay if I didn't have any kids.

Rationally I knew this wasn't true. I knew I was worthy as a human no matter what I achieved. But there was another part of me that didn't fully believe it. When even part of you buys into the lie that your achievement makes you worthy, then you work pretty damn hard to prove you're enough.

I was proving myself to compensate for my weight, being single, and not being a mother, but this wasn't actually about weight, relationship status, or motherhood at all. Most of my coaching clients are mothers and they, too, drive themselves to achieve in the same way I did, but for different reasons. Some of them even extend their drive *to* motherhood, constantly feeling behind in that arena as well.

Let's take Jessica. She came to me because she wanted to slow down, work smarter, and start enjoying her life again. She was married and a mom to two girls under the age of four. She had hustled in her business for years and consistently served her clients at the highest possible level—often too high. It had paid off financially, but it was taking a toll on her emotional life. She felt like she couldn't say no to anyone. She was the go-to in her office for advice, committees, and testing anything new.

Jessica was also driven in her personal life. In one of our first coaching calls, she assigned herself several categories of goals with multiple tasks in each category. She literally gave herself gold stars when she accomplished those tasks (and there's no harm in that—reward yourself in the way that works for you!). She had goals to start exercising, lose weight, drink less, go to church, and buy a new house—all while saying she wanted to slow down.

One day I asked Jessica directly, "What do you get from all this achieving?"

She blurted back without a moment's hesitation, "If I achieve, people will like me."

There it is. *The* reason that Jessica was working so hard. Jessica's inner critic told her that she needed to keep achieving to prove she was likable, which is really just another way of saying she was proving that she was worthy of being loved. So of course she was going to continue to work her tail off! We all want to be loved. We have a deep desire and need for acceptance and belonging. When we believe those things are dependent on achievement, then we will do just about anything to keep achieving.

You know it's not true. You know that the good people in your life will love you whether or not you make partner, earn six figures, or run a marathon. The problem is it *feels* true. The inner critic goes wild in your head and encourages ridiculous behavior to prove your worth. The inner critic tells you:

People will like you if you take on this extra work.
You don't need help from anyone.
You better show them what you're worth.
You'll prove yourself once you get the promotion.
You can slow down later.
If you say no, you'll let everyone down.
Keep working hard and they'll always need you.
If you aren't successful, what will you have to show for yourself?
It all has to be perfect.
If you rock the boat, they won't want you around anymore.
If you just work hard enough, eventually you'll be free.

There's one common thread between all these inner critic thoughts. One root cause lying beneath everything. The *one* thing you're really trying to prove: *you are enough.*

I'm here to tell you the inner critic is wrong. You are enough without the accolades. You are enough without the praise and recognition. You are enough without having to achieve anything at all. You are enough without the perfect presentation and the highest rating on your performance review. You are enough to be loved no matter what.

When you don't fully believe in the deepest part of your bones that you are enough without having to *do* anything, then you have to prove yourself over and over again. It is never enough. *You* are never enough.

You are on a constant hamster wheel to prove your worth.

If you slow down and take it easy, the inner critic flies right back in, waves its finger, and orders you to pick up the pace.

Before you can let go of the expectations of the inner critic, you need to understand *what* you are proving. Your story may be similar to mine. You might be overcompensating in your work to make up for places you feel behind personally, like being single or not having children. You might be like Jessica, who worked to prove she was likable through achieving.

Your reasons might be completely different as well. You might be married and have kids, but not feel great at home, so you put too much energy and worth into work because you know you can be successful there. You might be proving that you're needed, that your company or clients or colleagues can't live without you. You might be proving that you can hack it on your own, that you don't need help from anyone.

Or it might be something entirely different from what I've mentioned here. The point is, you need to figure out what it is for you. You need to understand what you are trying to prove through achievement so that you can let go of hustling for your worth and instead strive in healthy ways to create impact and have personal fulfillment.

Discover what you are proving

Give yourself at least thirty minutes to complete this reflection. It's better to use a pen and paper instead of a computer, if you can. Not only do ideas flow more naturally through writing, but you also won't be tempted to stop writing to check your email or Instagram! If you hate writing, you can also speak your responses into a recording.

Remove as many distractions as you can and give yourself the space to dive deep into this exercise (and all the exercises in this book!). This exercise may be uncomfortable, and, when anything makes us feel vulnerable, our natural reaction is to look for distraction to stop the discomfort. Silence your phone and put it in another room. Shut yourself in the basement, den, or even your bathroom if that's the only place you can get privacy. Tell your partner that you need some time alone.

If pain or discomfort comes up during this exercise, embrace it. They are just a signal of something that needs to be explored and healed. Write about what you are feeling instead of avoiding it. Digging through the discomfort is where the real change happens.

1. Set a timer for fifteen minutes. If you must use the timer on your phone, flip it over once you hit start to avoid distractions from pop-ups.

2. Journal your response to the question, *What am I proving by achieving?*

3. Write continuously for fifteen minutes. Don't pause. Don't edit. Write down any thought that enters your mind, even if you don't like it. Don't worry about punctuation or spelling or even making sense. The purpose is to get everything down on the page, and writing continuously helps uncover things hiding in your psyche that you aren't consciously aware of.

4. When the timer goes off, take a deep breath (and wring out your hand—it will probably be a little sore!).

5. Read through what you wrote. Underline anything that stands out to you.

6. Write down the insights you gained from this exercise in your journal. What did you learn about what you are proving through achievement?

It is common for deep realizations to arise from this exercise. If you find that you would like more support, reach out to a coach or therapist to help you process what you are discovering.

CHAPTER TWO

whose rules are you following?

In April 2018, Intertwine, my spiritual community, took a collective day of no obligation. Rest was the main objective, and I could choose what that looked like to me. It was a day to unhook from work and social media and follow exactly what my heart and body told me to do.

I knew I needed this day. I was just a few months into running my business, and I had barely taken a full day off since I started. For entrepreneurs, there are no boundaries, except the ones we enforce on ourselves. Which, as we've already established, I haven't always been great at doing!

This is one of the reasons the day appealed to me. It wasn't just a commitment to myself, but to the community. Others were also taking a day of no obligation, and I liked being in on it together.

The day of no obligation was the first truly nice day after an exceptionally long, horrendous winter. We are known in Minnesota for having hard winters, but this one had been over the top. We had two blizzards in April. We got so much snow that I cross-country skied right out my front door down the middle of my Minneapolis street during one of them. Robins that had flown in thinking spring had arrived huddled together on tree branches heavy with snow.

It had snowed over a foot just a week before the day of rest, but the weather had turned quickly and most of the snow had melted. The forecast was sunny and sixty-five glorious degrees. This is equivalent to nirvana for Minnesotans in April.

Every part of me ached to be outside in the sunshine. I laced up my waterproof hiking boots, drove the fifteen minutes from my condo in the city to suburban French Regional Park, and got out on the trail.

It was amazing to be outside. The sun actually felt warm on my body. Birds chirped all around me. I could sense the whole world coming alive after the long winter.

Parts of the trail were still covered in snow, but that only added to the fun. I slid and slipped and laughed my way through the mud and slush around the three-mile loop. It was pure joy.

After hiking for an hour, I reached the end of the loop. I paused for a second and immediately thought to myself, "I have time—I *should* do another loop."

Then I caught myself. This was my day of no obligation. I didn't have any "should" today. I asked myself the real question:

Do I actually want to hike another loop?

The answer was a clear *no*.

I had loved the first loop and it was time to be done. I didn't need to do another loop just because I had time. I got to choose.

I realized that day I was following a rule for exercise: more exercise is always better. When given the option, I should always choose more exercise. I should always do the extra ten minutes on the elliptical trainer, always go for the walk, and always do the second hiking loop.

I also realized I didn't need to follow this rule for another second.

This unnecessary rule I carried around for thirty-seven years originated in two places—my family and the beliefs of my younger self. Everyone in my family exercises all the time. Some are pretty hard-core about their exercise (my aunt runs ultramarathons, my sister-in-law qualified for the Boston Marathon her first time ever running a marathon, and my brother had done several century bike rides), but it's more that we *never stop moving*. My dad will play eighteen holes of golf in the morning and then go for a fifteen-mile bike ride in the afternoon. My mom will spend hours gardening, meet a friend for a walk, and then run up to the YMCA to lift weights. And then they'll both go for a walk together after dinner. We all learn by example, and my family taught me that exercise is not optional and whenever you have free time, it's a good idea to fill it up with movement.

My younger self also created this rule separately from my family culture. I mentioned in the last chapter that I was overweight for much of middle school, high school, and college. For years, I punished myself for overeating by trying to burn all the calories I had consumed. I remember a time I stayed on the elliptical machine at the gym until I had burned a thousand calories. My journals from middle school have entries detailing how long I spent on the NordicTrack and the number of calories I had burned. There were days I spent ninety minutes on that fake cross-country ski machine in the basement.

There are a lot of wonderful, healthy aspects to this rule. While many people struggle to keep an exercise habit, that's never been a problem for me. Even during the busiest, most stressful times in school and work, I always made time for exercise. It kept me sane. It's also allowed me to do things I really love, like taking a fifteen-mile hike on vacation in Patagonia. I'm grateful my parents instilled this habit in me from a young age.

Aside from the benefits, you can see the dark side to this rule I followed. Not only did I use exercise as a punishment for eating when I was younger, but I felt guilty for *not* exercising—even when it would have been better to rest. I exercised through illness and exhaustion and pain. I got mad at my muscles when they were tired and I didn't think they should be. Because I kept exercising when I should have rested, I injured myself further. I've had tendonitis in my hand, wrist, elbow, shoulder, and hips. I've gone to physical therapy more times than I can count.

I have no interest in giving up exercise. I love to move my body. It brings me joy and clears my head. There's nothing better than going on a long, hard hike.

But I didn't want to feel like I had to exercise when I knew it would be better to rest. I didn't want to feel guilty for choosing to not work out two days in a row (heaven forbid!). I didn't want to hurt myself further by going too hard.

It was time to write a new rule for myself. Not one that served my family. Not one that served my younger self.

A rule that served me, right now, at this point in my life.

The unwritten rules of our lives

We all follow rules. It's efficient to follow rules. They create a shortcut in your brain so you don't have to think—you just do. Some of those rules are healthy and functional and cause us only good. You learned to brush your teeth twice a day as a toddler and that's a good one to keep following!

Some rules may even be empowering and motivating. If you learned that you could be anything and anything was possible, regardless of your background, then you're going to be more likely to put yourself out there and go for big things. If you learned that everyone was creative in their own way, you will express your creativity with greater ease.

Other rules get in the way of your success and happiness. They are often so engrained in your psyche that they become a blind spot. They are running inside your head on autopilot, governing your decisions and behavior and you don't even realize what's happening. These rules are buried deep in your family stories, in the cultural expectations that have surrounded you since birth, and in the fears, hopes, and dreams of your younger self.

Think back to the poem I shared in the introduction. Reading it now, I see rules I wrote directly into the poem, but didn't notice at the time. I literally wrote the words, "Failure is not an option for me." Think of the stress caused by following that rule! I studied and worked so many extra hours to ensure I followed this rule.

This rule is also categorically untrue. Failure isn't just an option—it's a requirement to reach your full potential. Without failing, you'll never know how far you can go.

Failure means you're pushing the limits, trying new things, and being creative, but it's hard for overachievers to accept.

The unwritten rules you're following may be completely different from mine. Here are some of the common rules that show up in my clients. They don't often recognize they are following these rules, but they are there, a conductor in the background of their life, guiding their actions and decisions.

I can't slow down because things will fall apart.

I'm not the smartest one in the room, so I have to work the hardest.

I always have to do my best.

I have to reach the goal I set for myself in college.

I can't say no or they won't want me around anymore.

I shouldn't show people what I'm good at—they will think I'm arrogant.

I can't disappoint anyone.

I should just be grateful for everything I have.

I have to put my family first.

I can't change my career.

I have to be productive all the time.

I can't share my ideas until they are perfect.

Do you recognize yourself in any of these rules?

Another name for these rules is limiting beliefs. They are exactly what they sound like—beliefs you hold, often unconsciously, that limit you from fulfilling your potential, following your authentic path, and enjoying life. They affect your relationships, work habits, self-worth, finances, and health. They are *everywhere* in your life.

These beliefs served you at some point in your life. They helped you feel accepted by your family or friends. Following the rules gave you recognition and validation. These rules also protected you from shame, failure, and rejection. They covered your vulnerability and shielded you from pain.

Any person or situation can influence your limiting beliefs. The teacher whose name you can't even remember, but you know exactly when she called you bossy and you've been working to avoid being called that word ever since. The presentation in high school when you froze in front of the classroom and you labeled yourself as a bad public speaker so you'd never have to feel that embarrassment again. The time you tried out for choir and the director looked at you funny, and you immediately thought it was because you had a bad voice, so you dropped out of choir and didn't sing solo in front of anyone for years—even though you *loved* to sing. (Can you tell that last one is real?! I remember it as if it were yesterday.)

While one-off situations can leave a big impression on us, the bigger rules that govern our lives typically come from three main sources: family, culture, and your younger self.

Family

Close family members are the first influence in your life. From day one, they teach you which behaviors are acceptable and which are unacceptable through their smiles, comments, tone of voice, rewards, and punishments. Their actions, what they fought about, and how they criticized themselves and others all influence your beliefs, both limiting and empowering.

Overachieving is no different. If your parents told you to always try your hardest no matter what, you may now take that to the nth degree, even in situations that only require 80 percent of your effort. Anne, a super-high-achieving friend of mine, told me recently that her husband didn't really understand her constant need to get things done until he spent a weekend with her family. He noticed that Anne's family *never sat down*. He was ready for nap time, and they were ready to check the next item off their to-do lists.

No one told Anne that she couldn't ever take a break. No one directly said that it was bad to rest or slow down. They didn't need to say the words—they showed it every day in their actions. Constant movement was the norm in Anne's family growing up, and so it continued to be her norm as an adult. There are many times this approach benefitted her, like when she launched her business alone and had a million things to do to get it off the ground. There are also times it would have been better for Anne to stop moving and take a nap.

Movement and checking off the to-do list were Anne's filter of what was normal, so she never questioned her approach until her husband shone a light and helped her see she'd been subconsciously following a rule that may not always serve her. I have no doubt you are following family rules that don't always serve you either.

Culture

The expectations created by our national culture influence our rules almost as much as our families. Let's face it, in the United States we're taught every day that we are worth what we achieve. We are told to *do* your best—not *be* your best. Hustle is revered, especially among entrepreneurs. Perhaps you have seen the mugs that say, "Coffee. Hustle. Repeat." That's a clear message coming at you every day. You'd have to be made of iron not to absorb some of it!

Social media isn't helping. Social perfectionism—the kind of perfectionism where we feel like we have to meet others' expectations—has risen 33 percent since 1989,[1] and researchers think social media is partly to blame. You now get notified every time someone gets promoted on LinkedIn. Sure, it's a great opportunity to congratulate them. It's also a great opportunity to feel behind. We see the highlights of others' lives and compare them to the whole of our lives. This creates unwritten rules for how our lives and work should be.

Last year, I visited my then four-year-old niece, Linden, in Richmond, Virginia, where she lives with my brother and sister-in-law, and her older brother, Jack. I walked into the kitchen during my weekend visit to find her coloring at the kids' bright orange-and-yellow plastic picnic table. Linden *loves* art. She has more patience for art than 99 percent of kids. She'll sit for hours coloring and painting.

---

1 Thomas Curran and Andrew P. Hill, "Perfectionism Is Increasing Over Time: A Meta-Analysis of Birth Cohort Differences From 1989 to 2016," Psychological Bulletin, 145, no. 4 (2019).

On this particular day, she was filling in a coloring sheet with crayons. "What are you drawing?" I asked.

"It's from the grocery store. If I bring it back, they'll put it up on the wall."

What a great idea, I thought to myself. Such a fun way to display kids' art and make them feel good.

And then she said this:

"It has to be perfect so it can go up on the wall."

Perfect. Linden was four years old and already she thought her work had to be perfect before it could be shown in public. I immediately fast-forwarded twenty years into the future and saw Linden in the workplace, believing her new idea or project or presentation needed to be perfect before she could show it to anyone.

I assured Linden her picture didn't need to be perfect. I will continue to affirm her and every other little girl I meet that nothing about them needs to be perfect. They can experiment and play and have fun. They can share their half-baked, imperfect ideas with the world.

It's no one's fault that Linden believes her work has to be perfect. Subconsciously she picks up the expectation from everything around her. Our culture tells her to be cute and perfect, and rewards her well when she fulfills her role. It does the same for you.

Younger self

Your earliest limiting beliefs come from culture and the people closest to you. As you get older, you integrate new rules based on the expectations you hold of yourself. These rules are certainly influenced by family and culture, but they are more internally driven. My own overachiever behaviors are a great example. No one in my life ever told me I had to be the valedictorian or I wouldn't be loved or worthy—either directly or indirectly. No one told me I had to be the best and couldn't fail. No one punished me if I got a B on a test. I went to an elementary school where we didn't even get grades!

I still piled on the internal expectations. I created rules for myself and I followed them. Although I always enjoyed learning and doing well, these rules really began to take shape at the end of ninth grade when I saw my report card and realized I was ranked first in my class. I created a new standard for myself in that moment. A new bar that no one cared about except me. A new set of rules that influenced my life for over twenty years.

Expectations of your younger self often get in the way of following your authentic path. At some point in your early years, you created a vision of what life "should" be. If you're an overachiever or perfectionist, that vision likely included a dream of making it big in your career, in addition to the house and family and body and vacations you were "supposed" to have. As you move in the direction of all the things you were supposed to want, it's common to realize your goals don't represent the person you really are. Instead of leading to happiness and fulfillment, the rules of your younger self have left you burned out, disconnected, and questioning what you really want in life.

This is *terrifying.* When running toward goals is all you've known for your entire career, they become part of your identity. Even entertaining the idea of letting go of your goals can bring up a million questions and insecurities, most of them centered around the question "*Who am I?*" Who am I if I don't make partner? Who am I if I'm not married by twenty-eight and having kids by thirty? Who am I if I quit the job I thought I wanted, to do something else that might not even work? Who am I if I end this relationship? Who am I if I don't have a big corporate title to tell people when they ask me what I do?

I'll tell you who you are. You are *you*. You will be even more of you when you let go of the rules you've been following, whether they came from your younger self, your family, our culture, or anywhere else. Limiting beliefs steer you away from your true inner voice and your authentic path. It's not easy to get underneath them and understand all the unnecessary beliefs guiding your life, but it's well worth it. Your happiness depends on it.

• • •

Keep in mind that while it's important to identify your limiting beliefs and what caused them, it's also important to forgive. It would be easy to blame your parents and judge yourself for your limiting beliefs and all the ways they've held you back. Remember your family members operate under limiting beliefs as well. They did the best they could with what they had at the time. So did you. Forgive them. Forgive yourself.

One of my favorite Maya Angelou quotes is, "When you know better, you do better." This applies to all of us. You are taking the initiative to learn about yourself by reading this book. And now that you know better, you can do better.

Get clear on the rules you're following

Identifying the rules you've been obeying is one of the most important exercises in this book. They are the biggest reason you expect yourself to be perfect and overachieve, and have a hard time letting go of mistakes. They are the driving force guiding you to push yourself so hard. If you don't get to the root cause, all you're doing is putting a Band-Aid on it. No matter how many self-help books you read, coaches you hire, or yoga classes you take, if you don't change your rules, you'll always be fighting a losing battle.

Once you identify and change your rules, however, it *will* be easier. It takes work. Changing the beliefs you've held for thirty-plus years doesn't happen overnight, but the outcome is 100 percent worth the effort. Think of it this way: if you believe something needs to be perfect before you share it, it's *always* going to be stressful to share something, no matter how many times you've edited it, because you're human and it will *never* be perfect. If, on the other hand, you believe that progress is better than perfection, you will not only share your work faster, but it will be less stressful because you aren't expecting perfection of yourself.

Stop and think about these two beliefs right now:

- Everything has to be perfect before I share it.
- Progress is better than perfection.

Doesn't the second one feel so much better? Like you can heave a huge sigh of relief because the rule of perfection is gone? This is what it's like on the other side of your limiting beliefs.

You likely already started to identify your personal rules by reading through the examples in this chapter. To get even more clarity on your rules, observe your thoughts and actions over the next week. Notice what your inner critic says to you. Pay attention to every time you feel a "should" coming on. The messages of the inner critic and your internal "shoulds" are great indicators of the rules you follow in your life. Write down two to three observations in your journal each day for a week.

After the week is up, look back at your inner critic thoughts and "should" moments. Underline anything that stands out to you. What patterns emerge? What rules are you following? Write down your core rules in your journal.

Now go back through this list of rules and put a star next to the rules you need to release. These are the rules driving the perfection expectations you hold yourself to and causing you to hustle for your worth. These beliefs provoke you to take on extra projects and feel guilty for saying no. They hold you back from reaching your true potential and enjoying life.

In part two of this book, we'll work on reconnecting to your true self, the self that knows what is best for you and doesn't need to continue operating by the rules you've been taught. For now, observe how the rules you've identified show up in your life and know that you can change these rules. You don't need to keep operating within the system you were taught. You get to make up your own rules.

CHAPTER THREE

the benefits of your burnout

Let's take a step back—to the first semester of my sophomore year in college at the University of Wisconsin. I hadn't been able to maintain the straight-A status I had in high school, but I was still putting massive pressure on myself to do well.

My grades felt especially important this semester because I was applying for an amazing—and competitive—program abroad, studying tropical ecology in Costa Rica (did I mention that my undergrad degree is in conservation biology? Clearly, I didn't know what I wanted to do at that age!). Only thirty students from across the country were selected to join the program. This was the first semester I was taking classes in my major, so they would be pivotal in deciding if I got in. For the first time in my life, I applied to a backup program, just in case I didn't get accepted to the program.

Adding to this pressure was the fact that many of my classes were with premed students, and they were competing for much more than a study abroad program. The fight for As was fierce.

Finals started the third week in December. It was the heart of winter in Madison. The days were short and the wind was strong. I hunkered down in the library to study for hours and hours. I made flash cards for every concept and process from my intro biology class and recited them back to myself in my dorm room.

Just as my finals kicked off, I got what I thought was the flu. I had a temperature of 102, but you can't call in sick for your finals, so I bundled up and walked to my first final in Environmental Conservation. This was my easiest class of the semester and I wasn't worried about this particular final. Biology and environmental law were a little iffier, but this class? I felt good. Except for the fever, of course.

In the middle of the test, I suddenly got lightheaded and broke into a cold sweat. My eyes blurred and black spots swam across my vision. I felt sweat stream down my back and stick to my heavy winter sweater. I pushed the test aside, closed my eyes, and laid my head down on the desk. Part of me thought I should get help, but I felt like I would pass out if I tried to get up. Another part of me wanted to open my eyes, push through, and be done with the test.

Luckily, the symptoms subsided after several minutes. I raised my head, picked up the pencil, and finished the test. And I got an A, of course.

My other finals came and went without this level of drama, but the fever persisted for the entire week. I pushed through the chills and showed up to my finals with Kleenexes in hand, hoping I could hold it together and complete the test. I wondered what sickness I had that wasn't too terrible, but also didn't seem to be getting any better after days of feeling under the weather.

The answer came two hours after my last final, when the fever disappeared and I felt completely fine.

There were no germs in my body. No virus had taken

over and caused the fever and near blackout during my finals. It was entirely stress. It was a result of the expectations I had put on myself that I *had* to get into this study abroad program and I *had* to have top-notch grades in order to do that.

Here's where the paradox comes in. I *did* get into that study abroad program. It was phenomenal. One of the best experiences of my entire life. My fellow students were amazing. I felt like I'd found my soul mates. We camped in the rainforest all over the country and saw parts of Costa Rica that few humans get to see, let alone tourists.

Looking back, I can see that I studied too hard. I have no doubt I could have spent less time in the library and put less pressure on myself, and still gotten into the study abroad program. At the time, however, it felt like all that studying and pressure was necessary. Because I did get into the study abroad program, it strengthened the belief that I needed to drive myself into the ground to achieve what I wanted.

Fast-forward several years. I left behind my conservation biology degree and got a master's in human resource development. I started working in my first corporate job, coordinating global leadership development programs. I was twenty-eight and, in many ways, my career was just starting.

I loved my job, but it was full of a million details, and it felt like they all had to be perfect. I was responsible for all the logistics of getting groups of senior leaders from across the globe to the right place at the right time every time. I had to know every plane, bus, and car schedule. Every menu. Every approved wine. Every customer name. I was responsible for every slide deck and piece of paper handed out to every participant. And I was doing half of it in Spanish.

In the month before a program in Mexico, I had nightmares that I'd forgotten some critical detail and we'd left someone on the side of a street corner in Mexico City. I worried that one of our planes wouldn't show up and we'd be late and everyone would get mad at me. Not only did the stress keep me up at night, but I was completely exhausted with the sheer quantity of work I had to get done—and the ridiculously high expectations I held for myself and believed others were holding for me as well.

On our last day in Mexico, I almost fell off my chair right in the middle of a customer presentation because I was so tired. I could barely keep my body upright. I slept the entire flight home and another thirteen hours the night I got back.

But just like getting into the study abroad program in Costa Rica, I was again rewarded for my drive. I got a huge amount of recognition and credibility from working my tail end off. Senior leaders knew who I was and trusted that I could take anything thrown at me. I got a raise. Suddenly I was seen as someone with "potential."

It becomes a reinforcing pattern. You hold yourself to perfection standards. You drive yourself into the ground to meet those standards. You wake up in the middle of the night worrying you've missed a step. You stress eat. Have an extra glass of wine at night. You're exhausted and burned out, but no one sees you sweat, at least not at work.

Then your results are excellent. You exceed expectations.

Others recognize you. They praise your efforts, happily surprised at the amount of work you can complete at such a high level of accuracy. It makes you feel good about yourself.

So you do it all again the next time around.

Not only do you expect yourself to continue at this high pace and quality, but you've now trained others to expect it of you as well. I was in a meeting with a senior leader who said the reward for doing a good job at that company was they give you another job—without taking away the first one. This is what happens! You get more work piled on, and you continue to be great because the possibility of failure is unacceptable and, let's be honest, you like the rewards. It quickly becomes a vicious cycle.

The list of rewards from overachieving, perfectionism, and drive is long, and they aren't all bad. There's a line between healthy achievement and unhealthy "I have to prove myself and drive myself crazy" achievement. The problem is we often shoot way past that line and keep going until we are exhausted, sick, and soul-tired. Knowing the rewards feeding your overachieving will help you identify that line and pull yourself back when you cross it.

Here are the most common rewards for overachieving. See if you recognize yourself as you read through them. They won't all be major drivers for you, but I'm guessing one or two will stand out as motivation for your overachieving.

Praise, recognition, and validation

Who doesn't like to be praised and recognized? Even if you feel like you shouldn't like it because that would be arrogant or ego driven, there's a part of you that loves it. Sure, you might have preferences about *how* you're recognized, like not wanting to be called out in front of your whole team, but generally it feels great to know someone else sees and appreciates your hard work.

There's nothing wrong with this. There's nothing wrong with enjoying praise. Your great work should be recognized.

You cross the line when you start to rely on praise for validation. It's too much when you *require* outside recognition to say you're doing a good job and you fear you're failing when you don't receive that recognition. It's equally detrimental when you seek out particular work because you think you'll do well and be praised, instead of pursuing work that feeds your soul. This is when the overachiever gets out of balance.

Tara Mohr writes in her wonderful book, *Playing Big*, that praise is the cherry on top of an already delicious ice cream sundae. The sundae is delicious on its own and doesn't need the cherry, but it's a nice, enjoyable treat. If praise feels like the sundae itself, that's a clue your overachieving is driven by a need for validation.

Pay, promotions, and potential

If you're an overachiever who also has a skill for telling people about the great results you're getting, you are likely getting paid for it. Literally. A friend of mine working in medical device marketing got a spot bonus of several *thousand* dollars at the end of a particularly crazy project. During my compensation review after the six weeks of chaos that ended with me almost falling out of my chair from sheer exhaustion while in Mexico, not only did I get a raise, but my raise was made *retroactive* to the beginning of my tenure in the role. During the biggest, most stressful project of my life, the one that gave me shingles, I received gift certificates to a local theater and spa, and an iPad for personal use. These are very real rewards for driving yourself into the ground.

Then there's "potential." This really only applies to people in large organizations, but if you work at one of these companies, you know exactly what I'm talking about. When you work like crazy, take on more and higher-level work, get great results, and have a good manager or sponsor who is advocating for you, you get put into the "high-potential" category. With this designation comes opportunities for leadership development programs, interesting and challenging projects, work assignments in foreign countries, coaches, and accelerated promotions.

These are all good things—as long as you don't bury yourself living up to the expectations of being "high-potential." And as long as you actually want the opportunities you're being offered.

(Side note: There are also many overachieving women who toil behind the scenes, keeping their head down and hoping someone will notice and promote them or give them a raise. They work hard, but they keep quiet and don't share their accomplishments with the people who influence their career advancement, so they aren't rewarded for their efforts. There could be a whole separate book just on this topic.)

Avoiding failure and shame

It seems strange to call "avoiding failure" a benefit of achievement, but it underlies so much behavior that it has to be called out. Fear of failure is the root of perfectionism. It is the reason you read an email eight times before sending it and proofread a PowerPoint until you're blue in the face. It's one of the reasons you pull out your computer to answer email after your kids have gone to bed. It can keep you in unhealthy work situations and cause you to say yes to everything piled on your plate.

I spoke to a woman recently who left a bad job over ten years ago and still felt like it was a failure. She had always been the achiever and the good student. Her dad even told her that anything she tried just seemed to go well. And that was true—until this job. It was a bad fit for her personally and professionally. She quit after five months. While she *knew* it was the right decision, that feeling of failure still lingered years later.

For many of us, feeling like we failed brings on shame. If only you had tried a little harder, worked a little more, done something a little different, then maybe you would have been successful. If only *you* were a little better, then you would have been able to figure it out.

It doesn't matter how many times people say that failure is the way to innovation or that every experience is just learning, no matter the outcome. If you believe that failure means you're not enough, then you will do everything you can to avoid that feeling.

Identify your costs and rewards

Now it's your turn to reflect on what you gain from being the overachieving-valedictorian-perfectionist—and what it's costing you.

1. Fold a sheet of paper in half. On one side, write the headline "Benefits" and on the other side, write "Costs."

2. Start with the benefits. Write down everything you like about being an overachiever. Everything you gain from your inner valedictorian. Do you love praise? Have you gotten unique opportunities in your career? Do you like being seen as the person who is successful and gets things done?

3. Move to the costs. How does perfectionism and unnecessary overachieving impact your life? Do you get sick? Does it impact your spirit? What about your relationships?

4. Look back on your lists. What do you notice? Overall, what are you gaining and losing from overachieving?

CHAPTER FOUR

i've got this

When I was a leadership development coordinator, one of the first programs I organized was a weeklong session that took place in both Minneapolis and Houston, where our group of senior leaders was set to work with a customer. I had no idea what I was doing, but I muddled my way through the details. I organized three private planes to transport us between the cities (we couldn't fly on one commercial flight because we had so many critical leaders traveling that the risk to the company was too great in case the plane were to crash), memorized the group and individual transportation schedules for every member of the group, including our CEO, and handled all the materials. In the lead-up to the event, I woke up several times in the middle of the night after having nightmares that I'd forgotten some important detail of all the comings and goings of this trip.

Despite my nerves, all thirty-five of us arrived in Houston without any issues. The bus driver who picked us up from Sugar Land Regional Airport drove us for thirty minutes in the opposite direction of our hotel, but no one blamed me. People were shockingly calm about the whole thing.

When we finally arrived at our hotel, the driver unloaded everything from underneath the bus. Everyone had luggage, but I also had all the course materials for the week. More than one person offered to help me, but instead of simply saying, "Thanks, that would be great" and handing them a box, I chose to sling my backpack over my shoulders, balance one box on top of my roller bag and drag it behind me, and situate another box on my hip with my arm slung over the top, my fingertips barely reaching the bottom of the box. I was also carrying a large fake check that we were going to present to our customer with a donation to one of their favorite charities as a thank-you for hosting us. I have no recollection how I carried that as well, but it fit in there somewhere.

It would have been *so much easier* to accept help. I didn't even have to ask for it—it was offered directly to me. However, my lifelong MO has been "I've got it," so that was my response. I even took a certain amount of pride walking into the lobby of that hotel laden down with all my supplies without dropping anything. There was a kind of smugness about it. It gave me confidence to know I always had it together and could do anything on my own. I didn't need help from anyone.

My coaching client Kaia also had a lifelong history of taking on too much and never asking for help. She worked full-time, had two little kids, served on the board of a nonprofit, and helped with her son's Boy Scout troop. She was constantly behind, running from commitment to commitment without space to breathe. Much of our coaching focused on getting in touch with what she really wanted and valued in life—and learning to say no to everything else.

Kaia got really good at consistently saying no. She paused before saying her typical automatic yes to everything. She followed through on her goals to not make any new long-term commitments. It helped free up physical space in her calendar as well as mental and emotional energy in her head. This was step one.

Neither of us realized what step two would be until Kaia's car broke down and she had a board meeting that she had to attend after work. She plotted out the route on the public bus from her office to the meeting and arrived without too much inconvenience.

At the end of the meeting, a fellow board member asked Kaia if she wanted a ride home. As much as Kaia had an automatic "yes" for *giving* help, she had an automatic "no" for *receiving* help. She declined the offer.

Kaia left the meeting and started walking to a different bus stop from the one she used to get to the meeting. She soon realized the stop was further away than she anticipated. Not only that, but Kaia had to walk along the shoulder of a busy road to get there. So there she was, cars zipping by her at fifty-five miles per hour, walking quickly to find the stop where she would have to wait further for the bus that would bring her home. At best, this was unpleasant. At worst, potentially dangerous.

All of this when someone had offered to give her a ride.

It was a pivotal moment. We've all had them. They are the situations that hold a mirror up to your face and you immediately realize it's time to make a change. They are the flashes of insight that tell you loud and clear you no longer have to operate the same way you have been. You can tell yourself a different story about needing help and doing it all on your own.

Like Kaia, you are a smart, high-achieving, successful woman. You're holding a million pieces of life together, juggling twenty balls and keeping them all airborne. You can spill your coffee down your shirt and walk into a meeting with your CEO twenty minutes later. You can simultaneously make dinner, teach fourth-grade math, and listen to the emotional drama of a thirteen-year-old. You can leap tall buildings in a single bound. Possibly even walk on water.

In other words—you've got this.

But, also like Kaia—you don't have to.

The desire to do it all on your own is another piece in the puzzle of how you got here. The two examples I shared here are small, but you know it's not just about denying help once. It's the hundreds of times you say, "No thanks, I've got it." They add up and create layers of unnecessary tension, stress, and anxiety.

It's not only about accepting help with your suitcase or carrying the groceries. It's working late nights to complete a project that was really too much to take on in the first place. It's bearing the weight of your husband's illness in silence because you don't want to be a burden on anyone. It's crying in your car while sitting in the garage at home and then wiping your tears and smiling as you walk in the door.

You can do it. You've always done it. But you don't have to.

It's not that easy, though, is it? Why do we put ourselves through doing so much on our own when we could simply ask for help and make it easier? I see three overarching reasons.

You don't want to be a burden

This is *huge*. There is often serious guilt around asking for help. You're afraid you'll put a significant inconvenience on someone if you ask for their assistance or even just say yes when help is offered. You look around and see that everyone is just as busy as you are, and you don't want to add anything else to their plate.

This is the inner critic talking. It says, "Who are you to think your problem needs attention? Look at all the big things happening in the world. Be grateful for what you have and just get it done. Don't trouble anyone with *your* troubles. They have enough troubles of their own. You don't need to complicate their lives or bring them down with what you're going through. You don't want to make people feel guilty for saying no, so just don't ask at all."

This is just another case where the inner critic is lying. The truth is people *want* to help. They *love* to feel needed. This past winter, I moved out of the condo where I had been living for ten years and into my parents' house for three months while I looked for my next place to live. I didn't really want to pay for professional movers twice in a three-month period, but I also didn't want to be a burden on my friends. Saving money won, but I felt weird sending the email request out asking for help—even though I had helped some of the people on the email move themselves!

My friends *showed up*. They emptied out their cars and came prepared to haul everything across town. They carried couches and tables and chairs. They took my direction about where things should go when we got to my parents' house.

I gave them bagels at the beginning and beer at the end. That's it.

You aren't a burden. No more quid pro quo is needed other than bagels, beer, and a sincere thank-you. It doesn't matter if the people you're asking for help are friends, family, colleagues, or just an acquaintance that you ask for a ride home so you don't have to walk along a highway to wait for a bus. You're giving people the opportunity to help you. Let them.

You're following an unwritten rule

Yes, we're going back to the rules again! Part of this rule is habit; you don't accept help because you've never accepted help. You're like me—your MO has always been, "I've got this."

Your habit came from somewhere, though. You probably saw your mom running around like crazy to make sure everything was taken care of when you were a kid. When everyone else sat through dinner, she got up every five minutes to get salt or check on dessert or grab an extra napkin. You learned early that the woman's role is to take care of everything and hold it all together, so you continued the tradition without even realizing it.

It's not just our mothers that taught us. We get the message every single day that women are the caregivers, the nurturers, the glue holding the family together. According to the 2017 Bright Horizons Modern Family Index, even in partnerships where men take on half of the household responsibilities, women still carry more of the mental load.

Women are the ones who remember to put their kid in a lion costume for animal day at preschool. Women have their entire family's schedule plotted out in their heads and are constantly orchestrating all the moving parts to ensure everyone gets what they need.

Single women, don't you worry—this impacts you as well. I recently commented to a friend that I didn't experience as much of this mental load as mothers. While I do believe mothers experience this on a whole different level, my friend immediately pointed out that I do the same thing with my coaching clients. I carry all their details and emotions in my head in a way that most male coaches I know simply don't. They just let it go.

Most people reading this book grew up in an era where you were given the message that you could do it all. You could pursue any career you wanted. The glass ceiling was yours for the breaking.

Over the decades, we continually acquired new responsibilities, goals, and dreams, but we didn't take anything off of our plates. Expectations for what a woman should be didn't shift; they just got bigger. We created a new standard without letting go of the old one.

Not only that, but the expectations that you should always have it all together have become more visible as well. You see every family's perfect photo on Facebook, the amazing Pinterest unicorn cake, the highly Instagrammed two-week solo trek your single friend is doing in New Zealand (That would be me. I'm your single friend doing that.), and all the professional promotions and successes on LinkedIn.

There's another reason you're not asking for help as well.

This one is often hiding below the surface, lurking and snaking around in the dark because even admitting that it might be true makes you vulnerable.

When you ask for help, your entire persona as an overachiever that always has everything together is put into question. When you accept help—and especially when you actively *ask* for help—you admit that you can't do it all. Your ego doesn't like it. Cultural messages repeat that you *should* be able to handle it all. The Superwoman in you wants to be the one saving the day, not the one needing to be saved.

You've been programmed to believe "I've got this" is the best response to everything in life. It's a deeply engrained habit and automatic reaction. It can become another rule you're following without even realizing it.

What if they say no?

What if you gather up all your vulnerability, put yourself out there to ask for help when you really need it, and they say no? Or worse, what if they don't even respond?

I get uncomfortable just writing these words. Writing them down brings up fear in me, and I know I'm not unique. This is *all* humans at any age. The possibility of rejection is a hit to your core, a threat to your need for belonging. When you ask for help, the awkward teenager inside of you can come out strong. She goes into protective mode and tells you to do anything to avoid the possibility of rejection.

So you stay quiet. You keep your burdens to yourself. You show up in Superwoman mode, taking it all on and responding with a quick, "I've got it," whenever help is offered.

You probably even get recognized for your strength and ability to seemingly do it all.

In reality, everything you're taking on becomes layers covering up your true self. Your need to do it all on your own takes you further away from your core self, your true inner voice. It's one more piece of the puzzle of how you got here.

Notice how you respond to help

This coaching exercise is simple. Make a note of your response when people offer to help you. How often do you respond with your version of, "No thanks, I've got it"?

Get curious about what's going on beneath that response. Is it just habit? Are you following an unwritten rule that women always have to be the caregivers holding it all together? Do you feel guilty accepting help? Are you worried about putting a burden on someone else? Is it hard to admit you can't do it all? Write down your responses in your journal.

CHAPTER FIVE

two kinds of imposter syndrome

Soon after I started my business, I saw a pesky little thing getting in the way of many of my coaching clients in career transition. They came to me saying they felt stuck in their career and weren't sure what they wanted to do next. They wanted to be thoughtful and purposeful in their next step.

Through our coaching, however, I realized this wasn't actually the problem for most of these women. It wasn't that they didn't know *what* they wanted to do. It was that they didn't think they *could* do what they wanted to do. They worried that their success was really because of the company they worked for and not their own abilities. They questioned whether they had what it took to go for a director-level job, switch industries, or leave their corporate career and start a business.

Let me tell you—these women were amazing. I had worked with many of them previously and even called some of them friends. I knew they had fantastic experiences and qualifications and would be an asset to any organization. They didn't need to have every detail of their new job mastered on day one. I was confident whatever they didn't know when they started, they would figure out along the way.

While these women weren't aware of what was going on, I was. It was imposter syndrome.

I'm sure many of you have heard of it. Maybe it's a new

term for you, but you're going to know exactly what I'm talking about as soon as I describe it.

Imposter syndrome is feeling like a fraud or like someone is going to find you out, even though you are qualified. It's having a suspicion that one day, not long from now, everyone is going to realize you've just been fooling them, and they're going to tap you on the shoulder, tell you your time is up, and escort you out the door. It often shows up in how the inner critic talks to you, saying things like "You're not ready. You don't belong here. It's already been done—why even try? You're not enough of an expert to do that. Just who do you think you are?"

The crux of imposter syndrome is assessing your skills, qualifications, and experiences as less than they actually are. It's underestimating yourself. And it strikes highly qualified, successful women more than anyone. (Valerie Young's book on imposter syndrome is even called *The Secret Thoughts of Successful Women*!)

Despite its name, imposter syndrome isn't actually a syndrome. It's not a psychological diagnosis. It's something you *experience*, not something you *have*. People's experiences with it fall across a wide spectrum. Some people never experience imposter syndrome (lucky them!) and others experience it every day. (I had a woman in a very senior position at her company tell me that every day on her way to work she thinks, "Today's the day they realize I'm no good and let me go.") Many of us are somewhere in the middle, where certain situations or people trigger imposter syndrome, but you don't feel it all the time.

Once I realized that so many amazing women were being

impacted by imposter syndrome, I knew I had to do something about it. I immediately started talking about imposter syndrome on social media and pitching imposter syndrome workshops to organizations. A few months into working on imposter syndrome, a woman from the University of Minnesota reached out to me on LinkedIn. She managed a leadership development program for tenure-track professors (read: everyone in the program would have a PhD) and wanted to discuss a possible session on imposter syndrome for the group.

I happily got on the phone with her. I had done several workshops for different organizations by this point, and they had gone really well. People told me how great it was to know imposter syndrome was a real thing. They didn't feel alone anymore. Even better, they knew what to do the next time imposter syndrome showed up so that it didn't have to hold them back.

At some point during our phone call, as she told me about the group and what they were looking for in the session, she said, "We don't usually hire external speakers, but this topic is so important for our group that we really wanted to hire an expert."

Expert. That word flooded my body from head to toe with imposter syndrome. My inner critic went wild. "You're not an expert in this! You don't have a PhD! They all have the PhDs. They're experts—not you."

I was able to tame my inner critic enough to accept the opportunity, but the imposter syndrome was still raging. Despite having facilitated multiple successful sessions on imposter syndrome already, this one felt different. I suddenly had to *prove* I was an expert. I had to show up knowing exactly what I was talking about, being able to answer any question they could throw my way, and showing them every step of the way that I belonged there teaching them about imposter syndrome.

I started to look up journal articles and include academic references in my slide deck. I considered taking out a visioning exercise I had recently started using that had been very powerful for people because I thought it might be too woo-woo for a group of academics. Every action was taken with an underlying anxiety and fear they would find out I wasn't actually an expert.

And then I caught myself. I saw myself in the trap of imposter syndrome and I stopped. I reminded myself that the people in this workshop were just people. They may have had PhDs, but I knew more about imposter syndrome. Moreover, I knew how to teach them what to do when it showed up. I had valuable information to share and I was a good facilitator. I had the evidence from past workshops I had done. This group of professors was no different from anyone else. I told myself to connect with them as humans and forget about trying to prove myself.

My rational brain, the one free from imposter syndrome, was right. The workshop with the group of professors went great. I did the visioning exercise, the one I thought might be too out there. They loved it. It even brought one person to tears.

I've now led workshops on imposter syndrome with a few thousand people, and I've noticed people's reactions to imposter syndrome tend to fall into one of two categories.

They respond by either *underdoing* or *overdoing*. Underdoing includes holding yourself back from job opportunities, thinking something has to be perfect before you can show it to anyone, and stopping yourself from taking a risk because you don't think you're ready or know enough to handle it.

Overdoing is what I did. It's overpreparing and working like crazy to prove you're not an imposter and show everyone (and mostly yourself) that you belong. If you find yourself preparing for a meeting for two hours, and then find out a colleague only prepared for fifteen minutes and you performed the same, you probably fall into this category. If you read an email eight times before sending it, you're likely an overdoer. If you've ever uttered the words, or even had the thought, "I'm not the smartest woman in the room, but I can outwork anyone," then you fall squarely into this category.

You might also experience some underdoing, but I'm guessing most of you reading this book are classic overdoers. This goes straight back to the proving we talked about in chapter one. Imposter syndrome triggers you into overachieving, proving mode. If you feel like you're going to be found out for not being an expert or not being a real businesswoman, you're going to expend a ton of energy trying to fool everyone, to keep up the wool you've clearly pulled over everyone's eyes. If you don't fully believe you're qualified and deserve a seat at whatever table you're sitting at, then you're going to study and prep and know every detail to prove you belong.

Katie, one of my coaching clients, was a highly qualified HR professional. She had worked in nonprofit organizations for fifteen years in a wide variety of HR roles. She was interested in moving to the for-profit world and questioned whether she would have enough credibility to make that leap after so long in the nonprofit sector.

During our coaching, she got an interview for a great job. She fit all the qualifications to a tee, except one small area of responsibility—benefits. This was only 5 or 10 percent of the job, but Katie was so worried that she would be found out as not having enough expertise for the job that she studied for hours and hours before the interview, memorizing data on health plans and 401(k) matches. Even though Katie had every other qualification at the highest level, she focused on this one piece where she was lacking. It caused her to feel like an imposter applying for the role as a whole.

This is what imposter syndrome does to overachievers. It throws you into overdrive to prove that you know enough, whether you're interviewing for a job, sitting in a meeting with senior leaders at your company, or thinking about pitching to a dream client. Usually you do succeed, which contributes to perpetuating the cycle of overwork, burnout, and reward. Just like everything we've talked about so far in this book, imposter syndrome brings you further away from your true self and your authentic path.

Oh, and by the way—no one ever asked Katie about benefits in the interview. And she got the job.

A new kind of imposter syndrome

Everything I've described so far is the official kind of imposter syndrome. The imposter syndrome that was named in the 1970s and has been studied for years and years by psychologists. But I've noticed a new kind of imposter syndrome coming on the horizon as well.

This new version is less about feeling like an imposter in your *work* and more about feeling like an imposter in your *life*. It's the sense that you're not really following your authentic path. You might feel like you're meant for something more, even though you have traditional success. It might feel like there's something else inside of you just dying to get out, but you aren't really sure what it is. You get nudges that there's a different life out there for you.

But whenever these nudges come up, the inner critic asserts itself, saying you should be grateful for what you have, that other people would kill for your job and life. You're comfortable and not unhappy—isn't that enough? And what is this other path anyway? You aren't some hippie revolutionary. Stick to what you know.

Lauren and I started working together shortly after she attended one of my imposter syndrome workshops. She was a business owner and, instead of running her business, it was running her. She was working way too many hours, and it was taking a toll on her health. She wanted to reimagine her life and business and put a plan into place to move in the direction of happiness.

Lauren definitely identified with the traditional definition of imposter syndrome. There were times she questioned whether she knew enough to work with certain clients. She felt like others in the room were smarter than she was, even though she also believed she was great at what she did.

As we dug deeper into coaching, however, a new theme emerged. In her heart, Lauren was an artist. Although she had worked in creative fields her entire career, primarily in writing, she hadn't fully explored her artistic side.

For decades, Lauren denied the call to become an artist, professionally and personally. She had dabbled here and there, but never given herself permission to fully create art because she didn't think she was good enough. Lauren continued to listen to her limiting beliefs and inner critic instead of her true inner voice, and, over time, it slowly led her away from her authentic path. She felt like an imposter in her life because she wasn't fully expressing herself. She was holding back an undeniable part of her core from the world. Lauren constantly drove herself to be successful in her business, but all the achievement in the world isn't fulfilling when it's not aligned to who you really are.

I also ignored the nudges of my true inner voice for years. Although I enjoyed my jobs in the corporate world and have no regrets about my time there, I always felt like something was a little off. I'd tell friends and coaches I didn't think I was meant for a lifetime corporate career. I had little interest in being a top-level leader, even though people told me I had the potential to get there. I never voiced a direct desire to be an entrepreneur, but I wrote things in my journal like:

- Right now, I feel like I'm using my true self for very little. I'm fulfilling the expectations of my role, but I'm not living to a higher calling.

- I want to find energy from creating new things, contributing to a higher calling, and doing work for others instead of just trying to get as much done today so that there's less of it to do tomorrow. I don't want to just check off boxes. I want to create new things.

- Part of me has always felt like a fraud here. Like there's a piece of me bottled up and screaming to get out.

- Sometimes I feel like I'm living a fake life. Going through the motions, but not really going after anything.

- I'm tired. It's time for a vacation, a break to really get away mentally and physically, but it's also time for a real change in my life. Not a Band-Aid. Not a cover-up. Not trying a new hobby or focusing on weight or exercise to distract myself, but real change. A step toward returning to the full authentic me. I've somehow lost a part of myself and it's time to get it back.

This wasn't a one-time feeling. These journal entries were written on separate days over the course of two years. Part of me felt like an imposter during this time. I wasn't living a fake life, but I wasn't living one completely aligned to my personality, desires, and mission either. I had the nudges, but I chose to ignore them because it was easier to do that, at least in the short run.

You'll read more in the next chapter about how I reconnected with myself and stopped living a semi-imposter life, but for now know that two things happened at work that made me stop to do serious reflection on what I really wanted in work and life. First, my true inner voice stopped whispering and giving nudges and instead gave me a full-blown, screaming message that was nearly impossible to ignore. Second, my job changed to something I knew I would hate. I found out about the change while sitting in my boss's office the morning of my thirty-seventh birthday. I had to hold back tears when I heard the news. My entire body had a visceral reaction. I knew with 100 percent certainty this was not the job for me.

Those two triggers set me off on a journey to reconnect with my true inner voice so that I could get off the imposter path and get back to walking my authentic path. I started exploring entrepreneurship and almost immediately knew it was the right decision for me. Ideas started pouring out of me. My creativity shot off the charts. Amazing people showed up in my life and gave me advice, ideas, and resources for starting a business. It wasn't *easy*, but it was *right*.

The same thing happened to Lauren. She chose to adopt the attitude of an explorer and it led her to pair creative writing with photography. She also followed her true inner voice toward connecting further with nature and working on climate change, another area where she always had passion, but didn't give herself full permission to embrace. She doesn't know exactly where it will all lead, but she knows she's on the right path.

The official imposter syndrome still shows up for both of

us, but it's easier to combat when you don't feel like an imposter in your life. When imposter syndrome makes an unwanted appearance now, I know how to reconnect to myself. I slow down and listen to my body. I create and play and embrace wonder and joy. I remind myself of what success really means to me. I question my skills and qualifications less because I know myself better and have less to prove (ideally nothing to prove, but it's a journey! #workingonit). I'm learning to let go of expectations and live a life designed by my own rules.

In the second half of this book, you'll learn how to reconnect to yourself and live by your own rules, but before we move there, let's recap. Imposter syndrome has contributed to where you are in two ways: 1) When you feel like you're less qualified than you actually are, you're going to work like crazy to prove that you belong and that you're an expert, and to keep from being "found out" as a fraud. 2) When you consistently ignore your true inner voice, you pull further and further away from your authentic path, making you feel like an imposter in your life. Both cases hold you back from living to your fullest potential.

Pinpoint your imposter syndrome

This chapter's exercise is all about noticing. Don't worry about changing anything; just pay attention and observe how imposter syndrome shows up for you.

- Over the next week, notice when you feel like an imposter. Do imposter feelings show up around certain people, like leaders in your organization or when you think about contacting a big client? When you ask for money? When giving a presentation? When talking about your career goals?

- Reflect on the root cause of your imposter feelings. Is it the traditional imposter syndrome, where you're underestimating your abilities and feeling like you have to prove yourself to keep from being found out? Is it the new type of imposter syndrome, where you're feeling more like a fraud in your life as a whole? Or a combination of both? I recommend doing this reflection through journaling, but you can also reflect through quiet contemplation or talking to a therapist, coach, or trusted friend.

Don't worry about changing anything just yet. That is the work of part two. For today, just pay attention and reflect.

PART TWO

reconnect to yourself

CHAPTER SIX

reawaken your true inner voice (and release your inner critic)

We've talked a lot about the inner critic in this book. The inner critic telling you that you have to prove your worth through work. The inner critic repeating your limiting beliefs over and over until they are embedded so deep in your brain that you don't even notice them. The inner critic flooding you with imposter thoughts that you're not qualified and successful, even though that's exactly what you are.

The inner critic is such a relentless voice in your head that it's easy to mistake it for your own voice. We listen to the inner critic like it's speaking the truth. We believe its words. After all, if you hear something a million times over, you're bound to start believing it. And the inner critic is nothing if not persistent. It tricks you into believing it's the one and only truth.

Even though the inner critic is a constant companion, *the inner critic is not you.* Not even close.

There is another voice living inside of you. Your *true* inner voice. This is the voice of your inner wisdom and your inner knowing. It is your core self, your soul, and the center of your being. Reawakening this voice is the first step to reconnecting with yourself.

Let's go back to the story I started in the last chapter, the story about how I decided to leave my corporate job and start a business. You know the part about my job changing.

That was concrete and tangible. I was going to hate my job and that wasn't okay with me. Something had to change.

What you don't know is my journey to entrepreneurship kicked off a few months before my job changed—and in a way that wasn't concrete or tangible at all.

It was fall of 2016. I had scheduled a development conversation with my manager to talk about my goals and where I wanted to take my career. I knew the company I was working for wasn't a great long-term fit for me, but I loved my job facilitating women's leadership development programs and I liked my manager (we're still in touch!). I thought carefully about what I wanted to tell her about my career plans.

On the appointed day, I sat down in my manager's office and started telling her that I wanted to be a director, lead a team, and create strategy. In the middle of my carefully prepared script, a voice came to me and said, "*You are lying right now.*"

I had never heard a message so clearly in my entire life. It wasn't negative or critical; it was just *true*. I knew it with all my heart the second I heard it. I walked into that office knowing exactly what I was *supposed* to say. I thought it was what I wanted, but my true inner voice knew better.

I had no idea what to do with that voice. Unfortunately, there wasn't an accompanying statement that said, "And, by the way, you should start your own company, coach, speak, and write a book." Nope. That did not happen. But I knew I had to pay attention to this voice. I knew it was something important. I knew it was time to open myself to possibilities apart from the obvious path in front of me.

My true inner voice had woken up, and I was *not* going to tell it to go back to sleep. It was time to let go of the expectations of the inner critic and start following my own truth.

It's time for you to pay less heed to your inner critic and give more attention to your true inner voice as well. To do that, you need to be able to recognize the difference between the two. Let's get clear on how they each show up in your world.

The inner critic

In the broadest terms, the inner critic is the negative voice inside your head telling you that you're not worthy. Your inner critic can be critical, condescending, and just plain mean. It often gets repetitive, circling the negative messages around and around inside your head, driving you down into a self-doubt spiral. You know that one tiny mistake you made in a presentation last week and can't stop thinking about? That's your inner critic.

The inner critic isn't rational. It doesn't care that all the evidence in the world proves you are worthy, amazing, and wonderful. The inner critic only sees evidence of every part of you that is lacking. Every way you're not qualified. Every fear supporting its words. We often know the inner critic isn't *really* telling the truth, but it *feels* so true we believe what it says.

I call my inner critic The Valedictorian. She's basically all the parts of me that were exhausted and driven to the extreme in high school. The Valedictorian says that I won't be successful in my business until I've matched my corporate salary and then some. It says I need to prove myself. It sees all the people that appear like they are running über-profitable businesses and tells me I better hustle before I fall further behind. The Valedictorian says I need to be successful the first time I try something new or else I'm a failure. Indirectly it says that I'm not worthy unless I'm getting it all right and having all the success—and all on my own.

The weird thing about the inner critic is that it's just trying to keep you safe. As humans, we are programmed to be constantly scanning the horizon looking for risks and remembering every bad thing that's ever happened. Our brains automatically imprint anything negative so that we avoid it in the future and stay safe. This tendency even has a name: negativity bias.

This programming worked really well when we lived outside and had to be on alert to anything that could put our lives at risk, but it's become an overused skill. Think about the last time you were really nervous. Perhaps you had to give a presentation at work. Just thinking about the presentation made your palms sweat (maybe they are again right now!). Your heart pounded in your chest as you walked to the front of the room. You had a knot in your stomach. Your breath got shallow. Your face flushed red. Every signal in your body screamed, "Don't do this! It's not safe! Run out the door and don't come back!"

Now ask yourself a question: Were you safe in front of that room? Was there any threat to your life as you gave the presentation? No, of course not! Yet your body was having a *very* physical response. Your brain responded in the same way to that presentation as it would being chased by a lion. It sees them both as a threat, and it tells you, in no uncertain terms, to avoid that threat.

Your brain sees anything outside the status quo as a risk. Even when the status quo isn't aligned to your goals, dreams, or authentic path. Even when the "same" isn't particularly healthy. Your brain prefers the devil it knows to any unknown out there.

If you listen only to your inner critic, it will take you further and further away from yourself. Heeding the advice of the inner critic leads to anxiety, stress, and even shame. The good news is there's another voice inside of you. It's often quieter than the inner critic, but it's *powerful.* Once you start listening to this voice, you tap into a power you never knew you had.

True inner voice

Your true inner voice is the opposite of the inner critic. It's curious, compassionate, and kind. It may give you a kick in the butt occasionally, like when it told me I was lying in my manager's office, but it speaks from love, not shaming or contempt.

Your true inner voice knows you are worthy for who you are, not what you do. It has nothing to prove. It doesn't need approval or validation. Praise is just a bonus for the true inner voice. Criticism is merely feedback. Your true inner voice sees many options and paths—none of the black-and-white, all-or-nothing demands of the inner critic.

This is who you really are. Your core self. The true inner

voice is the part of you that has shed all expectations and exists separately from the inner critic. It's your values and strengths and everything that makes you amazing. It's humble and confident at the same time. It's the voice of your heart. Your knowing that just knows.

You might refer to your true inner voice as your inner wisdom, inner mentor, spiritual guide, or intuition. It may be your wise future self or inner child. Some people connect it to their religious beliefs. I prefer true inner voice and will continue to use this term in the rest of the book, but the name doesn't matter. Call it whatever makes sense to you.

I've already talked about my inner critic, The Valedictorian, but I haven't talked about my true inner voice. Her name is Radiance. Now before you think I've gone completely off the deep end into total woo-woo territory, let me tell you the origin of Radiance.

In 2009, I enrolled in coaching training through the Coaches Training Institute. I had always been interested in coaching, and my manager approved me to attend their introductory weekend workshop. During the three-day training, we learned to listen with focus, ask powerful questions, and connect to our core values.

This wasn't a sit-in-your-chair-and-take-notes-during-a-droning-PowerPoint kind of training. It was an all-encompassing, interactive experience. We observed a coaching skill and then practiced it immediately. Every person in the training both coached and got coached over and over throughout the weekend. It was massive skill building and intense personal development at the same time. I'm pretty sure everyone cried at least once during the weekend.

As part of the training, we did a future-self exercise. One of our trainers guided us through a twenty-minute visioning where we fast-forwarded ourselves twenty years into the future, to the home of our future self. I not only saw my future self and where she lived, but I got to have a conversation with her.

This visioning was ten years ago, and I've forgotten many of the specifics, but I remember exactly what it was like to be around my future self. She was full of light. She had a peaceful confidence about her. She was connected to nature and wearing feminine, flowing clothes. Nothing about her was manic or rushed. She knew exactly who she was and had nothing to prove.

At one point during the visioning, our leader guided us to ask our future self her name. Mine immediately responded with, "Radiance." It was the perfect name for her. She was radiant inside and out. Light poured out from her soul and overflowed to everyone around her.

As I said goodbye to my future self in the vision, Radiance handed me a glowing globe and said, "Bring your light and the world will light."

Ten years ago, and I remember that scene like it was yesterday.

Radiance isn't just my future self—she is my true inner voice. When I let go of proving and overachieving and the need to always be successful, she shows up. When I release my ego and instead focus on serving and loving and creating, that is Radiance. She is always with me because she *is* me. Sometimes I need to slow down and reconnect to her, but she will never go away.

Identify your inner critic and true inner voice

The Valedictorian and Radiance are my inner critic and true inner voice. Yours may be completely different. Later in the chapter I'll share a visioning exercise to identify your inner critic and true inner voice. I've done that visioning with over a thousand people and *anything* can show up. Here are just a few examples I've heard from coaching clients and workshop participants:

Inner critic	**True inner voice**
• A dark, stormy tornado	• Calm, peaceful, open prairie
• Bully from second-grade class	• Self as a little kid, playful and confident
• Overly critical father	• Self at age seventy-six, wise, confident, and peaceful
• An overweight guy sitting in the corner eating Cheetos and laughing at you	• Mom
• Medusa	• Wonder Woman

As you can see, a wide range of images come up for people! It's normal for your inner critic or true inner voice to be someone you know. Parents, teachers, and people from your past are very common. If that person shows up as your inner critic, it doesn't necessarily mean they are an awful person; it just means something in your experience with them resonates as your inner critic. It's also normal to see something weird and strange that makes no sense to you at all. Two different people in separate workshops have told me an image of a guy named Fred popped up as their inner critic—and neither of them even knew a Fred!

You might be thinking right now that all this seems pretty out there. I get it—and I will also tell you it works. When you create an image and character of your inner critic, it's easier to separate yourself from it. When your inner critic pipes up, you see that it's not *you* talking and you don't have to follow that voice. Instead, you can tell it, "Thank you, but I'm not listening to you today. Time for you to get out of the driver's seat and locked back in the trunk where you belong."

Similarly, connecting to your true inner voice allows you to tap back into that voice when you need it. Once you have an image of your true inner voice, you can consult with it. You can ask, "What is my true inner voice saying right now?" or "How would my true inner voice show up in this situation?" You can also use the feeling of your true inner voice to decrease stress and bring in calm and peace. Who doesn't need more of that?!

I've found that reconnecting with your true inner voice automatically decreases the volume of the inner critic. It doesn't go away entirely, but it's weaker. Your inner critic can't compare to the power of your true inner voice once you revive it.

Get to know your inner critic and true inner voice

The transcript for the visioning is written below. You can also find a recording of the visioning on my website at www.heatherwhelpley.com/book. Here are few tips to help you get the most out of this exercise:

- If you aren't able to access the visioning recording, have someone read it to you. You need someone to guide you through it—just reading the visioning won't give you many insights.

- The visioning itself only takes about five minutes, but allow yourself at least ten additional minutes to write down anything you want to remember from the visioning. Additional journaling reflection questions are listed at the end of this chapter. You can complete them right away or wait a few days and then journal.

- Set yourself up in a quiet place where you won't be interrupted. Hearing voices or other loud sounds will interrupt your thoughts and bring you out of what you're seeing in the vision.

- You can sit in a chair or on the floor or lay down for the visioning. Any position where you are relaxed (but won't fall asleep!) is good.

- The visioning will start with a short breathing and relaxation and then we will move into seeing your inner critic and true inner voice. Don't worry about how this will happen. I will guide you through the entire thing.

- Some people have significant insights from this visioning and others have small realizations. Let go of any expectations that you need to get all the answers from this visioning. Whatever comes up for you is right. There is no need to force anything.

- There will be times when I pause in the visioning. Keep your eyes closed and focus on whatever you're seeing in your mind. You'll know the exercise is finished when I ask you to open your eyes.

Start by getting comfortable. You may put both your feet on the ground and find a comfortable spot in your chair or you may sit or lie down on the ground. Close your eyes and take a few deep breaths. Feel the air pass through your nostrils, then down your throat, into your lungs, abdomen, and all the way to your lower belly. Then feel the air release from your belly, lungs, throat, and nose. As you breathe deeply, feel any tension melt away from your body. Relax your jaw and all the tiny muscles in your face. Let your shoulders drop away from your ears. Focus on your neck and back and let any stress you're carrying there just slide away. Continue to breathe deeply. With every breath, you release tension and welcome in relaxation.

I want you to start hearing your inner critic. Whatever negative things that voice tells you, bring them forward now. You're not qualified, you're going to fail, you have to work harder, it's already been done, you aren't creative—whatever the inner critic says to you, make it loud.

Now envision what that voice looks like. Give it a form.

Maybe it's a person you know, maybe a character, maybe another kind of form. What does your inner critic look like? What is it wearing? What is your inner critic doing? What's its name? Study your inner critic for a minute.

Now take a deep breath. As you breathe out, release your inner critic. Feel it melting away, disappearing into the distance. You start to hear a different voice. Your *true* inner voice. It's a calm, curious voice. It's the voice of your inner knowing, your inner wisdom. This voice is completely aligned with your values and purpose. How does this voice sound? What does it say to you? Now that voice comes close and you see that it has a form. Maybe it's a future or past version of you, maybe it's a character, maybe another kind of form. What does it look like? What does it feel like to be in the presence of your true inner voice? What is the name of your true inner voice? Study your true inner voice for a moment. What does your true inner voice want to say to you now? What do you need to know? Take a second to listen to your true inner voice. She may respond in words, a picture, or just a feeling. If you'd like to ask your true inner voice a question, do that now. Listen for the response.

Now see your true inner voice fading into the background. Know that your true inner voice is always there when you need it. Sometimes it only whispers and you have to listen, but it's always there to guide you. Take a few more deep breaths to come out of this visualization. When you're ready, open your eyes and write down anything you want to remember.

Go deeper

- Over the next week, pay attention to any additional insights you gain from the visioning. It's common for you to be in the shower or out for a run and suddenly know the meaning of an unfamiliar image you saw or understand the message your true inner voice gave you.

- Observe your inner critic. Notice when it shows up. Does it make an appearance around specific people? Or certain situations? Is the inner critic louder at work or at home? Let go of any judgment you have of the inner critic (or yourself for having these inner critic thoughts) and just be curious and observe.

- Further explore your inner critic and true inner voice through journaling. Here are questions to get you started:
    - How does the inner critic impact you? How does it make you feel? What does it push you to do? What does it stop you from doing?

    - What control is the inner critic allowed to have in your life? What boundaries would you like to place on the inner critic?

    - What is the feeling of your true inner voice? How does it feel in your body when you are connected to your true inner voice?

    - What does your true inner voice find most fulfilling?

- What really stomps on your true inner voice? What makes it angry, sad, frustrated, etc.?

- What does your true inner voice say yes to? What does it say no to?

- Create a visual reminder of your true inner voice. This could be something you make, like a painting, drawing, or collage. It could also be something you already own that feels very true to you and represents your true inner voice. Display it in a visible location in your home or workspace.

CHAPTER SEVEN

repair your pace

If there were one thing I could say to all my clients, to women everywhere, it would be this:

SLOW THE F DOWN

We never stop! Our bodies and minds are going all the time. We get on a racing treadmill the second we wake up, and we don't get off of it until we go to bed—that is, assuming you can put the worries and to-do lists aside long enough to give yourself a break from the chaos and actually sleep.

I call this manic mode. It's feeling like you can't slow down. Like there will never be enough time to get everything done, so you rush from place to place to check another item off a to-do list that never seems to get shorter.

One of my clients refers to this state as panic mode. Not an actual panic attack—more like you're operating in a mildly panicked state. Unlike a true panic attack that may come and go, you can operate in manic mode every day of your life—and many of us do.

As humans, we are meant to both amp up and slow down in response to what is happening around us. There are times when our bodies and minds should be operating on all cylinders. Your stress response kicks into high gear, releasing all sorts of chemicals to put your body on alert, ready to run away from a threat, protect yourself at all costs, and keep you safe. Your ability to do this keeps you alive.

Manic mode should be reserved for the occasional situation when you need to protect yourself or someone you love from a real physical threat, like the time your entire body reacted to get your child out of the way of oncoming traffic. You didn't consciously think about what to do, you just *did.* Everything in you surged to protect the person you love. You probably only noticed after your child was safely in your arms on the sidewalk that your body shook and your heart beat into your throat and you could barely catch your breath.

You aren't, however, meant to live at this pace every day. Low-level manic mode causes an underlying feeling of anxiety running through your body. It's the slight knot in your stomach you feel but can't figure out where it came from. It puts you on edge at all times and blocks out the airwaves from your true inner voice.

I first noticed my own manic mode a few years ago while running errands on a weekend day. Somewhere between the grocery store and making returns at Kohl's, I noticed my whole body rushing with an urgent need to get everything done on my to-do list. It was like there was a hamster wheel inside my chest, and I could feel it spinning faster and faster, whirring inside my body.

Instead of ignoring the feeling and rushing to the next task, like I'd done my entire life, I stopped. Literally. I stopped my body in the middle of running errands while standing in a crowd of people who were probably also unknowingly running around in manic mode. I took a deep breath.

Within a few seconds, my rational brain kicked in and said, "This is ridiculous. Nothing you are doing is an emergency. You don't need to feel this way."

I took another breath and let go of my manic mode. The whir of the hamster wheel in my chest began to quiet down. My heart rate slowed. The underlying anxiety pulsing through my body subsided. Manic mode melted away. I realized I could be productive and calm at the same time. Manic mode didn't help me get through my to-do list any faster; it just made it less enjoyable.

Getting out of manic mode isn't just about making your task list more tolerable. When you're busy all the time, you don't have the opportunity to reflect on who you are and what you really want in life. Instead, you put your head down and force your way forward on the same path because thinking about trying to do anything else is too overwhelming.

Repairing your pace is the essential next step in reconnecting to yourself. Slowing down opens up space for joy and creativity. It lets you focus and be present. It gives you the energy to choose to listen to your true inner voice over the voice of the inner critic.

There are three key steps to repairing your pace and reconnecting with yourself: noticing when you're in manic mode, giving yourself permission to move at a different pace, and embracing the vulnerability of slowing down. Let's dive deeper into each one.

Notice manic mode—and pull yourself out of it

You already heard how I experienced manic mode when I first noticed it—the hamster wheel whirring inside my chest, feeling like everything is going faster and faster, and I'm going faster right along with it. I also have a tendency to quite literally bump into things when I'm in manic mode. I can't tell you the number of bruises and scrapes that have been the result of manic mode!

What are your manic mode signals? They may be the same as mine or completely different. Here are the common signals I hear:

- Feeling like you're constantly rushing
- Noticing your body tilts forward to plow through to your next thing
- Doing everything fast—talking fast, eating fast, walking fast (you might even break into a jog moving between meetings)
- Realizing you haven't stopped to catch your breath—literally or figuratively
- Being unable to listen and be present with others because your head is so wrapped up in everything you have to get done

Once you know your manic mode signals, pay attention to them. Notice when you're in manic mode. You might be rushing between the tomatoes and bananas in the produce section of the grocery store, shoving lunch into your mouth at hyperspeed while prepping for your next meeting, or circling in your head with everything you need to get done instead of listening to your spouse.

Wherever you are, whatever you are doing, once you notice yourself in manic mode, *stop*. And then breathe. Take a deep breath way down into your lower belly. Feel manic mode loosen its grip. Release the parts of your body that feel tight. Notice your heart rate slow down. Sense the rushing wheel in your chest go back to a normal pace.

If you're not in a place where you can actually stop for sixty seconds, then force your body to move more slowly. My client Katherine often notices her manic mode between meetings, when she is power walking on her way to a conference room or taking the stairs two at a time. She makes her legs walk slower. She takes deep breaths and feels her body calm down.

This isn't natural for Katherine. She has to make the conscious decision to slow down in the moment. She tells herself that it doesn't matter if she walks into the meeting thirty seconds later. Part of her doesn't believe it. Part of her wants to go faster and rush into the meeting, but she knows it's better for her to slow down and get out of manic mode. She feels better when she slows down, and—bonus—she walks into the meeting with greater strength and charisma. (Did you know that people interpret moderately paced, purposeful movements as confidence and rushed or twitchy movements as lacking confidence? Keep that in mind if you need some extra motivation to pull yourself out of manic mode.)

If you're accustomed to moving through life in manic mode, it may take you a while to notice it. We're not used to paying attention to our bodies. In fact, most of the time we completely ignore the signals our bodies send us to slow down, until we are forced to slow down when we get the flu or a migraine. If you have a hard time noticing manic mode or listening to your body in general, no need to worry. We're going to talk more about reconnecting to your body in the next chapter.

Give yourself permission

Noticing manic mode and pulling yourself out of it are physical steps you take in the moment. Giving yourself permission to slow down is a mindset shift. One that is often harder than it sounds.

There are so many reasons it's challenging to slow down. Feeling guilty for saying no and setting boundaries so that you can slow down. A culture that tells us we are only worth what we produce. Social media and all the messages telling us to hustle 24/7.

For me, the biggest obstacle to slowing down is the driving need to achieve and get things done, even at home. Slowing down feels like accomplishing less—and that is terrifying and vulnerable for an overachiever.

I realized I had this limiting belief around slowing down after a mini breakdown on December 21, 2018. (I mentioned this breakdown briefly in chapter one as well.) I had a call scheduled at noon with Allie, my digital marketer. I came prepared for the meeting with a long list of questions to ask her so I could jump off the call and get right back into work. I had been going at a crazy pace for weeks with the goal of launching a program for the new year, and we were getting down to the wire. This was our final call before Christmas, and I wanted to get as much out of it as possible.

Instead of asking Allie the questions I had carefully prepared, I got on the call and collapsed. I started crying and couldn't stop. I didn't even know *why* I was crying. Nothing was particularly wrong. There was no single trigger, no one identifying incident that put me over the edge. Instead, I was overwhelmed with *everything*. I'd been going so fast to make my self-induced deadlines that I hadn't paused for weeks to ask myself how I was doing, and I couldn't take it anymore. Everything I felt came out in tears.

At the end of our call, Allie suggested nicely that I go take a nap. I had planned to continue working the entire afternoon, but I knew she was right. I crawled into bed at two o'clock, turned off the lights, pulled down my light-blocking shades (which were practically unnecessary on December 21 in Minnesota), and lay under the covers for the next three hours. I didn't even sleep. I just lay there with my eyes closed in the quiet. I gave myself permission to take a three-hour break from thinking and manic mode and pressuring myself to get everything done and just let myself *be*.

Those three hours allowed me to quiet my inner critic and get back in touch with my true inner voice. The voice that knew the world would not come crashing down if I missed the New Year's deadline. The voice that told me if this program failed, that didn't mean I was a failure. The voice that knew with certainty that I was worthy regardless of the conversion rate of my Facebook ads or how many people I added to my email list.

Allie gave me permission to slow down that day. If you also need permission, here it is: *I give you permission.* I give you permission to sit in your car for fifteen minutes and read before you pick up your kids from daycare. I give you permission to block your schedule for two hours and do whatever you want to do. I give you permission to say no, take a nap, paint, and eat an amazing piece of dark chocolate cake and savor every bite.

Here's your permission slip. Copy this page, tuck it into your wallet, and break it out anytime you need a reminder to give yourself permission to slow down.

PERMISSION SLIP

I, ______________________________,

give myself permission to ______________

____

____

____

____

Date ____________________________

Embrace the vulnerability of slowing down

This was the part I didn't realize for a long time. Yes, we are addicted to busyness. It's part habit, part cultural conditioning, and part limiting beliefs. All these things make it difficult to slow down. But there's another reason as well. One that's harder to admit to ourselves.

Slowing down is vulnerable.

When you quiet your mind, things surface you've been working to avoid. Emotions you've been pushing down show up. Questions you've been evading are suddenly standing right in front of you. You feel like everything is going to fall apart, like dropping one ball will cause all of them to come crashing to the ground. When you define yourself by your busyness and check marks on a to-do list, you question who you even are when you slow down.

Slowing down opens you up to all sorts of vulnerability. And that's hard and uncomfortable and something that's easier to avoid. So you stay busy.

Let's go back to my client Katherine, the one who had to consciously force her body to move more slowly and bring herself out of manic mode. Slowing down was incredibly vulnerable for Katherine. Every time she got quiet, she wanted to cry. There wasn't a specific reason that she was aware of, but something inside of her was touched deeply.

If you have this reaction, there's nothing wrong with you. Instead, it's a sign to slow down even more. Let go of any notion of transcendence or perfect quiet or the "right" way to slow down. Instead, muddle through it. Let yourself feel all the emotions you're feeling. Sit with them, process them, and eventually let them go.[2] Slowing down is hard, but when you notice your manic mode, give yourself permission, and expect vulnerability; there is magic in slowing down. It

---

2 If sitting with your feelings is too hard for you or past traumas come up, it may be a good time to reach out to a therapist.

opens you up to creativity and focus and joy. It helps you reconnect to your body. It allows you to be grounded and centered and present. It opens the airwaves so you can hear your true inner voice.

Create your own slowdown practices

The next step to rediscovering slowness is to create practices in your life that will enable you to slow down. These are activities, environments, and people that help you get centered, take a breath, and reconnect to yourself. There is no one right answer; it's about figuring out what works for you to slow down in the midst of your life.

As I read through my journals as research for this book, I noticed many entries over the years where I absolutely *craved* nature. I wrote about needing a place where I could hear myself think (basically the same as saying I needed to connect to my true inner voice), about wanting to be outside in the fresh air and sunshine, about my love of hiking and being in the woods.

Last year, I spent a day hiking alone in Maine's Acadia National Park before attending a business planning retreat in Portland. It floored me how quickly stress fell out of me once I got in the woods. Even though my body was moving, everything else in me was slowing down. Anxiety released every time my foot sank into the dirt. Every breath of pine air brought me one step closer to myself.

This is what you're looking for in your slowdown practices. You want to include activities that get you out of manic mode, take every drop of stress out of you, and slow you down. Creative practices, dance, music, meditation, prayer, reading, and time outside are all great ways that help many women slow down internally.

You can use these slowdown practices in two ways. First, build them into your regular schedule when you can. If you know that painting makes you feel amazing, create your own art corner and paint for thirty minutes before going to bed instead of watching TV. If you're like me and being outdoors keeps you centered, organize your social activities or exercise to take place outside. Meet friends for biking instead of a dinner out. Take your kids on a mini hiking trip at a state park.

You can also use your slowdown practices on an as-needed basis. If you notice you're in manic mode and can't pull yourself out of it, make one of your slowdown practices a priority that day. Once you know what works for you, this doesn't necessarily have to consume a lot of time. Fifteen minutes of reading, playing the guitar, or just sitting quietly might do the trick. Give yourself permission to take that time. It will be good for you and everyone around you.

A note about unhealthy coping mechanisms versus slowdown practices

Whenever I ask an audience for their preferred practices to get reconnected to their true inner voice in a workshop, someone inevitably calls out "Wine!" or "Margaritas!" While there is nothing innately wrong with having a glass of wine or a margarita for most people, I want to bring awareness to the difference between slowdown practices that get you back in touch with your true inner voice and unhealthy coping mechanisms that slow you down, but numb your real feelings.

The key is the feeling and drive behind the action—not the action itself. Watching an episode or two of *The Crown* because you love it is great. Watching an episode or two of *The Crown* to avoid emotions and vulnerability that come up when you slow down isn't great. Purposefully looking through Facebook or Instagram for fifteen minutes is fine. Scrolling mindlessly for an hour is not. Having a glass of wine and really enjoying it is satisfying. Relying on a glass of wine to calm you down is not.

Several years ago, I worked as an HR manager at a turkey-harvesting plant in Virginia for one summer. The HR team had lost both their supervisor and manager, and I was transferred there for a few months to fill in the gap until they found a permanent manager. The job was hard. I never knew what emergency might arise the next day, but I knew each day would be long. On top of that, I didn't have any friends in the area, so my usual balance of fun and work was completely gone. I no longer had anything to look forward to in the evenings or weekends. I learned a lot that summer, but life was not particularly enjoyable.

Nearly every night in Virginia, I stayed up way too late watching TV. It didn't matter what was on—reruns of anything mildly entertaining would do. I wasn't watching TV for enjoyment; I was watching it to stay up. I didn't want to go to sleep because that meant I would have to get up and start a new hard, long day. Instead of recognizing that feeling and dealing with it, I numbed it by watching bad TV.

You may already know the difference between the healthy slowdown practices and unhealthy coping mechanisms in your life, but if you aren't sure, ask yourself these questions:

- Does this activity make me come alive? Or does it dull me?
- Do I feel more in touch with my true inner voice while doing this activity? Or further away?
- How do I feel when I finish? Does it make me feel good (like really good—*soul* good) or do I feel blah or unhealthy?

Notice the differences for you and practice replacing unhealthy coping mechanisms with healthy slowdown practices. Embrace the vulnerability that comes up. If you can't let go of the coping mechanisms, I suggest reaching out to a therapist or seeking other professional help to understand what is happening for you.

CHAPTER EIGHT

return to your body

I was completely out of touch with my body for years. Even when I did hear a signal from my body, I tended to ignore it. Looking back, I can see the root cause was shame. I hated my body. I blamed myself for being overweight and unable to control myself around food. I was ashamed of the way my body looked and felt. It was easier to ignore my body than deal with the shame that came up when I did pay attention to it. (Remember that little note about coping mechanisms in the last chapter? Here it comes up again! Ignoring and denying are awesome coping mechanisms.)

Losing weight empowered me and made me feel like I could take control of my health, but it didn't reconnect me to my body. Instead of learning to notice my hunger signals and trust that I could follow them, I counted points and measured and logged what I ate. They were helpful tools, but the second I stopped using them, I would start to slowly gain weight. Every time.

Additionally, although I felt more confident in my body than I did when I was overweight, I still wasn't comfortable in it. I shied away from tight clothes, especially anything that might cling to my waist. Heaven forbid I would sit down and someone might see a roll around my belly.

It was more than just comfort with my body image. I actively fought against my body in so many areas of my life. I stayed up even when I was tired, until I was completely exhausted and had to crash. I pushed through hard workouts when my body screamed at me to stop and just take a nice walk outside instead. I got annoyed when I was legitimately hungry and didn't feel like I should be.

In short, I was living in my head. I needed to get back into my body and give it a seat at the table. It deserved a vote in my decisions.

Getting out of my head and back into my body has been a process. For me, it will be a lifelong practice of noticing and choosing to return to my body over and over. I still struggle with eating and, even though I love healthy food, I often overeat. Going to town on chips and guac at a party or eating a second helping of cake and ice cream brings back the feelings of shame fast. I still get self-conscious wearing tight clothes around my waist. It frustrates me that I still haven't figured this out, even after so many years of working at it.

On the flip side, I can see how far I've come. I legitimately appreciate my body now. I love its strength and how it can propel me up a hill while I'm hiking. I allow myself to take a nap in the middle of the day when I'm tired, even on a workday. When I'm truly hungry, I let myself eat.

It's more than just these concrete physical feelings. I *live* in my body more often now. I dance in my kitchen and notice the way my body moves. I feel my whole self as a part of that movement. I recognize my feet hitting the ground and how my hips circle as I move forward. I acknowledge how my body feels when I consider a decision and let it tell me the right answer.

Returning to your body is the next step in reconnecting

to yourself as a whole. Your body is a vehicle for your true inner voice. It holds wisdom and guidance. When you slow down and give your body a vote, it's easier to see when you are in driving overachiever mode—and it's easier to bring yourself back to you.

In this chapter, we'll go through several ways to get reconnected to your body. If you're like me and voted your body off the island years ago, it may be hard to tap back into your body. We're going to start small with these steps. No need to try all of them at once (I see you, overachiever!); instead, choose one that resonates and start practicing.

Notice your body

In the last chapter, we talked about paying attention to when you were operating in manic mode. If you've already started to do that, then congratulations! You are noticing your body.

Now it's time to broaden your noticing. Since most of us don't connect to our bodies naturally, it's helpful to have a quick check-in process that you can use throughout the day. Simply ask yourself:

- What is my body telling me?
- What does it need?
- What would feel good right now?

Check in with your body several times a day. You can

set an alarm or do it at each meal or every time you get up to walk to the bathroom. The point is to get in the habit of purposefully paying attention to the signals and messages your body is giving you.

Sometimes the answers to these questions are very concrete, like my body needs sleep or a salad or some movement. Other times the answers are emotional, like my body is telling me I need to speak up or that everything is aligned right now because of the calmness I feel inside my body. Any messages your body sends are valid.

The last question, "What would feel good right now?" is a great one for making small tweaks to connect you back to yourself and feel good more often. You may not always be able to do the first thing that comes to mind when you ask yourself this question. Going outside for a run in the middle of a meeting probably isn't going to happen, even if your entire body is telling you that a run would feel great. But what would feel good in your body in the middle of that meeting? Could you stand up or give your hand a little massage or sit differently in your chair? Notice what small changes feel good in your body.

These check-in questions are meant to be asked at any time during the day as a practice to get more in touch with your body. You can also use them when you actively notice something off with your body. It's an excellent chance to dig deeper and figure out the message your body is sending you.

For example, in 2019, I sold my condo and decided to rent for a while, partly to save money and partly because I wasn't sure where I really wanted to live. I looked for apartments and didn't find much that fit both my wallet and what

I needed as a business owner who worked out of my home. I finally found one apartment online, called the day it was listed, and got the first showing for the next day. I felt like I may have possibly found my new home! Then the management company called me back a few hours later to tell me it had been rented. The rental market was so tight that people were applying for apartments without even seeing them!

I finally found an apartment that was a little higher in price than I'd hoped, but everything else looked good. It had great light, the living room was big enough to accommodate my desk, and the location along the river in St. Paul was fantastic. I was afraid I would lose the apartment if I hesitated, so I told the rental manager I would take it right after he had shown it to me.

I noticed immediately that something felt off in my body. I couldn't explain it, but the unrest was there. The apartment seemed like the logical choice, but it didn't feel like the right one. Even after I'd submitted the application, I continued to search for apartments online, but I didn't see any. I felt like this was the best option, despite how my body reacted.

Six weeks later, I moved in. In the space of a few hours, problems in the apartment began to reveal themselves. Things I hadn't seen in the showing hit me in the face after I moved in, like the unbelievable amount of light that poured in through the windows at night and all the noise I could hear inside my apartment, from moving vans and garbage trucks outside my windows to dogs barking and vacuum cleaners whirring in the building lobby.

I literally felt sick to my stomach the whole first week after I moved into the apartment. The light and the noise bothered me, but I knew it was more than that. I didn't know the exact source of my unease, but my body was giving me all the signals that I was out of alignment.

I called a friend who is a trained coach, and we explored where these feelings were coming from and what they meant. Throughout the course of a one-hour call, we discovered that I have a deep attachment to value. Feeling like I'm getting my money's worth is very important to me. This apartment was already outside my price range, which made me uncomfortable, *and* it had all these problems that I didn't know about when I signed the lease. I didn't feel like I was getting my money's worth. I felt like I'd somehow been cheated.

This is the wisdom of the body. Even though I wasn't cognitively aware that something was off with the apartment, my body was fully aware. It was telling me to slow down and reconsider. It urged me to trust that I would find the right place for me instead of making a decision based on the fear that I might lose out on an apartment. My body was out of alignment because my values were out of alignment.

Six months later, I moved into a new apartment. It was in the same building, just four floors up. I felt happier and more settled into this apartment on the very first night than I did the entire six months in the previous place. It was quiet and open, and I felt like I could breathe. I knew the former apartment had impacted me, but I didn't realize just how much dissention was happening inside my body until it was gone. My body told me the first apartment was wrong. It now told me this one was right.

Start paying attention to the signals of your body. They're often easier to notice when something is wrong, but you will notice how your body feels when everything is right as well.

Get out of your head and into your body

What percentage of the time do you live in your head? Instead of being fully present in the moment, you're paying attention to all the thoughts crossing through your brain. You might be cooking dinner, but you're thinking about the meeting earlier that day, or the deadline you have coming up, or the annoying colleague who never stops talking and chews with unbelievable volume, or the bad grade your child got on his recent math test, or how the entire world is going to implode with climate change, racism, and unethical politicians.

Sound familiar?

Pause for a moment and really think about how much of your day is spent in your head. What percentage of the time are you living inside your thoughts? It won't be an exact response. Take a guess.

Is it 70 percent of the time? 90 percent?

There's nothing wrong with paying attention to your thoughts, particularly when it's purposeful reflection. At the same time, a lot of anxiety happens in your head. Your thoughts circle and spin around and around without anywhere to go. You get stuck in rumination and you can't get out.

What's more, living in your head takes you out of the present moment. When you're thinking about the next thing or the last thing, you aren't fully listening to the people around you. You can't relax into playing with your kids. You don't notice the amazing details happening around you, which in turn decreases your ability for wonder and joy (more on that in two chapters!).

On the flip side, when you're fully present, stress goes down. The inner critic gets quiet fast. When you're in your body, you know you're safe. You can look around and know that everything is good right here, right now. The thing ruminating in your head isn't actually here right now. You can deal with it when it does become present and real again.

Doesn't that sound like a better way to be more of the time? Let's get out of your head and back into your body.

To start, I want you to think of the times you *aren't* living in your head. When are you fully present and living in your body?

Several different activities immediately come to mind for me. Any hard exercise gets me there fast—mostly because I'm working my body so hard that I can't pay attention to anything else! If I'm sprinting in a spin class or hiking up a rocky hill, I am fully engaged in my body, focused solely on taking my next breath. I love it.

Dancing is another activity that quickly gets me out of my head. If I'm nervous or distracted before a big meeting or critical phone conversation, I'll turn on Ed Sheeran's "Barcelona" or Imagine Dragon's "Thunder" and just *dance*. I flail my arms and swing my hips and move in any way that feels good. Three minutes later, the nervousness is gone. The anxious energy swirling in my head has disappeared.

If I'm in the middle of a meeting and I can't get up and dance (although, really, wouldn't meetings be a lot more fun if you could?!), I take a breath. Not an ordinary breath, but a deep breath all the way from my nose way down into my lower belly. I feel the air move through my nostrils and into my throat, chest, upper belly, and finally down to my lower abdomen. I focus all my energy on the area around my uterus and moving air into that place. And then I release the air, feeling it move through my belly, lungs, throat, and back out my nose. Just one fully focused deep breath helps get me out of my head. The practice takes about ten seconds, you can do it anywhere, and no one will notice. I teach this to clients who get flustered in the middle of job interviews to help them return to their present, confident self. It's the perfect hack to get back into your body.

What activities naturally bring you out of your head and into your body? Here are several to start you thinking:

- Going for a run
- Playing with your dog
- Yoga, surfing, dance—any movement where you have to be aware of balance and where your body is in space
- Writing, especially flow writing where you start and don't stop
- Time outside, especially if there's a physical component, like hiking or skiing
- Physical intimacy
- Singing or playing instruments
- Painting, drawing, or other creative activities

Maybe your activity is on this list; maybe not. What works for you? Write it down in your journal now.

Doing more of these activities will train you to be present in your body more often. You'll start to notice what it feels like to get out of your head. You'll experience the difference in your body. Once you do that, you will notice the times you are in your head and be able to bring yourself back to your body. Sometimes by doing one of the activities you listed. Sometimes by checking in with your body using the questions from earlier in this chapter. (What is my body telling me? What does it need? What would feel good right now?) Sometimes just noticing you're in your head will be enough to bring you back to your body and the present moment. You'll find what works for you.

Use your body to make decisions

We've talked about noticing the signals your body gives you to indicate if something is misaligned with your values and true inner voice. You can take this a step further and tap into the wisdom of your body to help guide decisions in your life and actually tell you the right answer.

It's a simple process that I've used many times during coaching calls—and with myself! First, bring to mind the decision you're trying to make. This could be as simple as deciding to volunteer for a single event at your church or as complex as deciding on a job offer.

Next, close your eyes and picture yourself having said yes to that offer. See yourself volunteering at the church or actually in the job. How does it feel in your body? Make a mental note.

Now picture yourself saying no to that offer or making the opposite decision. You've declined the volunteering. Said no to the job. How does this feel in your body?

When a decision is right for you, your body typically feels *expansive*. You'll get a sense of openness and freedom. There might be some fear laced into the expansion if it's a big opportunity that's a little scary, but it still feels open, like the opportunity is full of possibilities. You feel alignment between your body, heart, and mind.

On the other hand, when a decision is wrong, your body *contracts*. Literally. Your belly clenches or feels like it's folding on top of itself. You may get a tightness in the pit of your stomach. The body feels stressed. Instead of open, your body feels like it's closing up.

Your body knows the right answer. We know that when we're born, but it's taught out of most of us as we grow up. You can unlearn this lesson and return to your body, though. The connection has not been severed. Like everything we're talking about in this section on reconnecting to yourself, it just needs to be strengthened.

Returning to your body isn't a one-time reflection. It's an everyday practice and conscious decision to give your body a vote in your life. When you lead with your body, the inner critic quiets and you clear the channels to your true inner voice. Returning to your body is returning to *you*. Plain and simple.

CHAPTER NINE

rediscover your creativity

I loved artsy creative work in elementary school. I looked forward to art class and getting to do whatever fun project our teacher had cooked up for us. I wrote crazy stories to match the pictures in *The Mysteries of Harris Burdick.* I painted giant flowers on the back of a poster board. I didn't care if it was good. I don't think it even occurred to me to judge my art.

Until middle school. Suddenly art wasn't about expression or creativity or having fun. Instead, art had rules. One of my first assignments in seventh-grade art class was drawing a self-portrait on a grid using a photo we had taken of ourselves. My drawing looked *nothing* like the photo. I hated it. I wanted to throw it away and never see it again, but that wasn't the plan. Instead, all of our drawings were displayed in the hallway, where six hundred kids would walk by them every day.

I didn't take another art class for twenty years.

(My art teacher was also the only teacher in middle school to give me detention, so that didn't help my perspective on art either.)

Although I continued to write throughout high school (mostly super dramatic poetry I hid in my desk at home), for whatever reason, I never considered that creative. I wanted so badly to be creative, though! I looked longingly at the artsy, creative drama kids in high school and wanted to be like them. They marched to their own drum and seemed a lot freer than I felt.

When I taught environmental education after college, I was surrounded by über-creative folks. Everyone had a nickname (I was Mortie). My friend Gladys (real name Jessie) wore a blue wig on a day trip to Boston, just for the fun of it. Chewy (real name Josh) and Eric (the only one of us without a nickname) spent an entire evening pretending to be Russian cosmonauts. No one was sitting around painting and drawing all day, but they just *screamed* creativity.

I could act in a skit with the best of them, but I didn't believe I had the creative flare of everyone around me. I loved to have fun, but I was more likely to follow the crazy than create it.

Both the desire to be creative and the belief that I wasn't continued right into my corporate career in my late twenties. I even put creativity on my development plan at work. I wrote SMART goals to increase my creativity (which might be the ultimate creativity killer), but it didn't work. I still didn't see myself as creative.

One day in 2008 changed everything. I was a coordinator for a global leadership development program, and I had an idea for a new weeklong session based on volunteer work in Latin America. I conceptualized the entire module to Ipek, my manager. I told her what the participants would do, how we would connect it back to leadership development and strategic goals, and the different types of projects that could work for the program.

Instead of giving feedback on my ideas, Ipek looked at

me and said, "Heather, you're always saying you want to be creative. This *is* creativity."

In that single second the world opened up for me. My entire mindset about creativity flipped upside down—and the belief about my own creative prowess changed as well. Just because I couldn't draw a self-portrait on a grid didn't mean I wasn't creative. There were a million ways to be creative! I just had to look for the evidence of my own creativity.

Once I recognized my creativity, I saw just how critical it was in my life. This first corporate job working with Ipek on leadership development was inherently creative, even though I didn't see it immediately. I regularly designed new curriculum and wrote communications for our programs. It wasn't completely free self-expression, but I definitely flexed my creative muscles on a regular basis.

When my job shifted into a project manager role for a leadership development conference, the creativity dropped to almost zero. Instead of designing trainings, I managed budgets and policed other people's task lists. My work life was dictated by email and spreadsheets. (This was also the project where I got shingles.)

An interesting thing happened during this time. When creativity dropped out of my work life, it picked up in my personal life. For the first time in years, I had a desire to write. Poems flowed out of me, seeming to come from nowhere. It was like the need for creativity had to be satisfied somewhere in my life.

While I became conscious of how important creativity was to me, for years it remained in the background of my life. It took the form of journaling and picking up my camera every once in a while to take pictures around my neighborhood. I always felt a pull to do more, especially writing, but I didn't make it a priority. I looked at writing classes, but realized that I would miss half of the sessions because of work travel, so I never signed up.

When I changed companies in 2015, I stopped traveling. I also started working a typical eight-to-five schedule and rarely worked nights and weekends, something I hadn't experienced in years. It was amazing! I had space to think and be. I wasn't constantly trying to cram everything in. I could sign up for something fun in the evenings and attend every single session!

Writing was at the top of the list. I signed up for a community ed class within walking distance from my condo. I loved it and signed up for another class the next season. Then I started a blog. A few months into writing the blog, I went on a bike ride with my mom through a town in Wisconsin called Wanderoos, quite possibly the best name for a town ever. I posted a few photos online, and my writing partner suggested that I write a blog about it. Instead, I wrote a silly poem called "The Jedi Kanga-Wander-Roo." That poem opened me up to a new world of children's picture books, which I spent over a year diligently writing in my free time. I'm not published, but I went so far as to query literary agents and attend a workshop for children's book writers in California. Now I'm writing this book. I also have the first chapter of a middle-grade novel written that I will return to after I finish this book. Pretty crazy considering I didn't believe I was creative for a few decades.

During this same time, my mom started getting into art.

I don't remember her ever doing anything artsy when I was growing up, apart from scrapbooking and the very occasional craft project. As she moved into retirement, however, she began taking painting classes. She got involved with the White Bear Center for the Arts, pouring wine at all their events (the perfect job for my extroverted mom!). Then she started to make things with clay. When my parents took up winters in Florida, she joined a local community art center so she could work with clay several times a week with friends. This past year, she had a booth at an art fair in their housing development and sold $500 worth of her clay work. She leads volunteer art projects with Ziggy's Art Bus, a mobile art experience for kids in hospice and long-term medical care, as well as a shelter for youth experiencing homelessness.

My mom inspired me to let go of my belief that I was "bad" at art and try things without worrying about the outcome. She brought me to classes on jewelry making and painting with alcohol inks. For a Christmas present, I enrolled both of us in a mosaics class.

While I had fun in these classes, they were few and far between, and I didn't seek them out—until a few months ago. I started having a strong desire to create art. Not writing, but *art*. I wanted to paint and make colorful pictures, and it was *weird*. The thing that had brought me shame for so many years became a pull so strong I didn't know what to do with it. After all, I had no actual skills.

I considered when art had been joyful in the past. When had it been true, complete fun? Three situations immediately came to mind: 1) Painting giant colorful flowers in sixth grade, 2) Alcohol inks (they felt like a science experiment!), and, 3) The mosaics class. I got totally lost in the moment arranging those tiles.

What if I combined all three? I had no idea what that would look like from a practical perspective, but I kept myself open to the possibilities.

I got my answer during a gathering with Intertwine, my spiritual community. The theme was "serious play," and we not only played with art supplies but also shared stories of play in our day-to-day lives.

In the middle of playing and chatting, I got an image in my mind of exactly what I wanted to create with my own art. The next weekend I took a trip to Blick Art Materials, and a lovely woman shepherded me around the store, filling my basket with everything I needed to create my alcohol ink painting collage. Bless her heart—she didn't even look at me strangely when I asked for tempura paints, even though tempura is what you do to shrimp and no one over the age of twelve uses *tempera* paints. She simply took me to the acrylics section where I picked out black, white, robin's egg blue, and dark purple.

One hundred and two dollars later, I left the store ready to create! I came home, taped a blue plastic tablecloth to the floor under a small folding table in the corner of the living room in my 850-square-foot apartment, ripped a sheet of paper from the sketch pad I'd purchased, squeezed out giant globs of purple paint into a white plastic dish, and got to work.

I had a picture in my head of what I wanted to make, but no exact plan. I chose to follow what felt fun. I dipped one of the larger brushes into the paint dish and laid down a soft swirl on the page. Then I painted another swirl. And another. And another, until the entire page was blanketed with deep purple swirling circles. I added a little white to the purple and accentuated the swirls to make the patterns more obvious.

I looked down at the paper. I *loved* it. I loved the texture of the paint and how I could create a sense of movement with the swirls. It was just like being back in sixth grade. I didn't care if it was good. My overachiever had exited the room. I didn't think about anything else while I was painting. I was entirely present.

I moved on to step two—the alcohol inks. If you aren't familiar with alcohol inks, they are the best beginner art project. It's basically like putting food coloring on tile or paper. There are techniques you can use (I don't know any), but even the people who really know what they're doing can't control the alcohol inks entirely. That's why I like it. There are no grid lines. No rules. It feels like a big science experiment that can't fail.

I dropped the inks onto a new sheet of paper and watched as the pinks, oranges, and yellows blurred together and created new colors and patterns across the page. Every once in a while, I dropped in a touch of green or blue just for fun. There was virtually no rhyme or reason to what I was doing, and I was giddy. Joy seeped out of every pore of my body.

A few days later, I came back to the now-dry sheet of alcohol inks and cut out stars of varying sizes. I didn't look at the colors. I didn't try to match or coordinate anything. I just cut. I arranged the stars in a gentle arch on the swirling purple sky, cut out small blocks from my sketchpad and drew a letter on each one to form the words "Choose Wonder," and pasted them underneath the stars.

It was exactly what I had pictured at the Intertwine gathering. Maybe even better because I loved the process more than I ever expected.

Brené Brown said on Elizabeth Gilbert's *Magic Lessons* podcast, "Unused creativity is not benign." For years, I repressed my creativity because of a false belief—and, in the process, I repressed myself as well. It's no coincidence that my journey to rediscovering my creativity has aligned perfectly with listening to my true inner voice. Creativity *is* the true inner voice. An expression on the outside of what the true inner voice is saying on the inside. It doesn't need to be "good." It just needs to be you, getting something inside of you out into the world.

Rediscovering your creativity

You've been reading my creativity story for the last several minutes, and I'm sure many of you are sitting there thinking, "That's all well and good, Heather, but clearly you *are* creative. You've written a book. You make art in your free time. You're creative. I'm not."

That's why this chapter is called *rediscovering* your creativity. I didn't believe I was creative either. You may not believe it in this moment, but let me assure you—*you are creative*. You are inherently creative, even if you never pick up a paintbrush or draw a picture. Creativity is your birthright. Your true inner voice is *dying* to be expressed. It's just blocked up with years of conditioning to believe you aren't creative. It's covered up by the message that creativity is reserved for a special few individuals with a talent for painting, clay, or photography.

It's not. Everyone is creative. Here's how you're going to rediscover your particular brand of creativity:

1. Look for the evidence
2. Lean into what is fun
3. Let go of the need for it to be good

Look for the evidence

For years, my inner critic told me I was bad at art. It said I would be embarrassed if I tried to make anything. It told me to stick to academics and sports, where I knew what I was doing. It let me know over and over and over that I wasn't creative. The problem was that my inner critic was lying (as it often does). The lies were trying to protect me from shame (as is also often the case). I didn't want to repeat the shame from seventh-grade art, so my inner critic convinced me to stay small and hide. I noticed all the evidence that I wasn't creative and completely ignored the even larger pile of evidence that I was creative.

Let's take an honest look at that evidence:

Evidence I'm not creative

- Was bad at drawing a grid self-portrait in seventh grade
- Painting and drawing don't come easily to me

Evidence I am creative

- Have been writing stories and poetry since I was a little kid
- Design new exercises for trainings, programs, and coaching clients all the time
- Have a good eye for photography
- Combine recipes to create new dishes (I can't *not* tweak a recipe!)
- Love making and getting dressed up in unique Halloween costumes (going as the song "She Don't Use Jelly" by the Flaming Lips was a favorite)
- Can always think of a question to ask (curiosity leads to creativity!)
- Always coming up with new ideas for my business

Look at this evidence. Even I am amazed at the lopsidedness of this list, and I'm the one who wrote it! It makes me wonder why I ever doubted my creativity and hid the expression of my true inner voice for so long.

I want you to do the same. Make two lists in your journal of the evidence you have on both sides of the argument—one list titled "Evidence I'm not creative" and one titled "Evidence I am creative." It will probably be easier to come up with the reasons you aren't creative—after all, your inner critic has been repeating the evidence for years. Dig deep on the ways you are creative. It doesn't need to be artistic. You might be super creative telling a story with a PowerPoint deck or spreadsheets. Or experimenting with new baking recipes. Or getting dressed up and playing make-believe with your kids. It all counts as evidence for your creativity.

Look back at your creativity list. Let it sink in. Let yourself believe all the ways you are already creative.

Continue to look for the evidence of your creativity in your day-to-day life. As you look for the evidence, you will also start to use your creativity more often. It's a beautiful upward spiral once it starts.

Lean into what is fun

Now that you've started to embrace the possibility that you might actually be creative, what do you do with it? Here's my simple advice: Do what sounds fun.

If you're so scarred by embarrassing creative attempts that you can't imagine anything creative being fun, look back to your childhood. What did you love to do as a kid? Did you play with Legos for hours? Make friendship bracelets? What art projects do you still remember from elementary school? What did you like about them? What classes were you interested in taking in high school, but didn't because you thought you wouldn't be good or your overachiever didn't think were "worth" taking?

Take a risk. Sign up for a class that sounds fun. Community education is a great low-cost and low-risk way to try something new. Recruit a friend if you don't want to go alone. If you're too embarrassed to try anything in public, go to an art supply store and experiment in the privacy of your own home.

Remember your creativity doesn't have to be artsy. You don't have to paint or draw or make anything out of clay, although I highly recommend it! Making anything new is creative. Lean toward what is fun and see what happens.

Let go of the need for it to be good

This past Fourth of July week, my four-year-old niece, Linden, and I decided to make alcohol ink paintings in my mom's laundry room, which tripled as her art room and Linden's bedroom for the week of her visit. Linden loves art and was an old pro at alcohol inks by this age.

A few minutes into painting, Linden looked at my tile. Then she looked back at her tile. Her lip started to quiver. "Mine's not perfect!"

Seeing the tears welling up in her eyes, I responded, "Nothing is ever perfect! That's part of the fun with art. You don't know how it's going to turn out. You just have to try it and see."

I'm happy to say the crisis was averted. The potential tears never fell. I started to play up risk-taking by dropping the alcohol inks on the tile with great flair and an animated voice, saying, "Should I try it? Do I dare?!?"

Linden caught onto the enthusiasm quickly, even throwing her hands in the air a few minutes later and exclaiming, "This is why art is so fun!"

Art is fun. When you let go of the need for your art to be perfect or good or even presentable. This isn't easy for the overachiever. We want to be good at everything we do. That isn't going to happen with creativity.

Creativity isn't about perfection. It's about process and curiosity and experimentation. It's about getting your true inner voice out. It's about tapping into a different part of your brain. Creativity ignites your soul and enlivens every other part of your life.

You never have to sell what you create. You don't have to share it on Instagram. You can throw it in the garbage when you're finished if you like. It's not about the outcome. It's about the being that comes from creating.

So when you're sitting in that painting class and feeling like a fool and totally regretting your decision to take a risk and embrace your creativity, let it go. No one cares if you're good or bad. You're not getting a grade. You don't need to be the valedictorian here. Lean into the fun, let it go, and rediscover yourself in the process.

CHAPTER TEN

reclaim your joy

Several years ago, I told my coach, Michele, "I feel like I have less joy in my life than I used to." I have zero memory of what else we talked about that day, but that comment is burned in my memory.

I am a person naturally predisposed toward joy. I'm an optimist. I love life. I believe life is an adventure. I'm a classic Enneagram Type Seven—also known as The Enthusiast. I have a custom end table in my apartment with the Émile Zola quote, "If you ask me what I came here to do, I will tell you. I came to live out loud." I even titled my eighth-grade autobiography project "Life as an Exclamation."

Even in the midst of all the pressure I put on myself to succeed in high school and college, joy was still present. I regularly laughed until tears streamed down my face. I had no problem playing imaginary games with the kids I babysat. I sang and danced and acted in skits while working at my church.

Somewhere in the middle of my corporate life, that innate joy and zest for life began to fade. I was still happy, but the overflowing, can't-contain-the-life-flowing-inside-of-me river of joy wasn't as strong. You might chalk this up to growing up, but I didn't buy into that notion. I knew my capacity for joy was just as high as when I was a kid—and I wanted it back. Full force.

I can't point to a single moment when my natural level of

joy flooded back into me, but I can tell you it's back. Instead of a eureka moment, joy has returned because I'm doing all the things we're talking about in this book—slowing down, getting reconnected to my body, rediscovering my creativity, and letting go of the hard-pushing overachiever that always has to be successful.

There's more to joy than just following the steps laid out in the other chapters of this book, however. Joy is the next level. It's more than happiness. In fact, coaching clients often tell me they reached out in part because they wanted more joy in their lives. They almost never use the word happiness. It's joy they want.

So what's different about joy? The dictionary definition is to experience great pleasure or happiness, but most people describe it at a much deeper level. I took a poll on Facebook of how people define joy, and here are some of their responses:

- The feeling of elevation when I forget that I'm in my skin and just be
- Giggling inside
- The ability to connect with the present moment in a profound way—and simultaneously feel appreciation, satisfaction, and pleasure
- Soul-deep smile
- Joy feels like floating; I feel joy when I'm doing something that is authentically me

- Being so overwhelmed with happiness that all the world lives in that moment

- Detaching from the ego

- Overflowing positivity during the simplest and most mundane times, like being ecstatic when I'm in the grocery store

- It's a light, bubbly feeling; it's a sort of "having fun and delighting in life" feeling

- The feeling of just being with whatever is—surrendering in the moment without trying to make it change

- It feels like aliveness, like I am full of life and energy

- Joy feels like openness and possibilities to me—a buzz, a high, a bliss

I define joy as a feeling more than anything. It bubbles up inside my chest, like a champagne bottle was uncorked and the effervescence of life is overflowing everywhere inside of me. Joy is complete presence. Everything is here in this moment. I'm not worrying about if my belly is too big or if people are going to think I'm being weird or all the ways I feel behind. Joy is aliveness and connection and surrender to the here and now.

Wonder and joy are inextricably linked for me. When I'm in a state of wonder, of awe—or recognizing the amazing in the world around me—I am automatically in a state of joy. The simplest things often bring a feeling that everything is wonderful and aligned and joyful—the way the setting sun hits the snow, a perfect song on the radio, great conversation with friends, or when an idea hits me that I just know is right.

When you're driving and pushing, and putting constant pressure on yourself, there isn't much room left for joy. Because joy happens in the present moment, you can't be worried about your to-do list or ruminating on what you did or didn't say in the meeting *and* experience joy at the same time. Joy does not exist in comparison or in running to keep up or in playing by the rules you've been taught. There is no joy in proving or hustling for your worth.

Joy is simple. It's alive. It's full of wonder and presence and connection. And it's time for you to get it back.

The earlier chapters in this section on reconnecting to yourself are also keys to reclaiming your joy. Chances are good that if you slow down, reconnect to your body, and rediscover your creativity, you *will* find more joy. You'll even see some similarities between the steps laid out here to reclaim your joy and suggestions in previous chapters. But just like joy is the next level, these steps are also the next level. You're building on what you've learned and reconnecting to yourself and your joy in a deeper way.

Minimize distractions from joy and get present

Last summer my niece and nephew, Linden and Jack, came to visit (this is the same niece who loves art that I mentioned in the last chapter). At ages four and seven, they were bundles of energy. Even though I sometimes wanted to distract myself from their chaos, I noticed I enjoyed them a lot more when I was completely with them. No phone. No TV. No distractions. Just us. They talked. I listened and asked questions and laughed at their hilarious comments. I got to know them better as the people they are becoming. None of that would have been possible while scrolling through Instagram or checking my email.

I am convinced presence is the foundation of joy. Look back at the definitions of joy people shared. They include words like "surrender" and "all the world lives in that moment" and "forget I'm in my skin and just be." You can't feel joy if you aren't present and connected to the here and now.

The challenge is that our world is designed to distract us from the present moment. Phone notifications. Multitasking. Responding to email while also getting instant messages. Eating while working at your desk. Reading a text while having a conversation with your spouse. I personally feel the worst when I've spent an evening watching TV with my computer open. I used to think it would make me feel better about working at night if I had something fun on in the background, but instead I felt unsettled and plain yucky. The opposite of joy.

You can invite more joy into your life simply by minimizing the distractions from joy. Your phone is the easiest place to start. Turn off the notifications. Delete social media apps and reinstall them for a set number of hours a day. Keep your phone in another room or hidden in your purse when you're out with friends. Resist the urge to scroll when you're waiting in line at the grocery store, watching your kid in the bathtub, or at a stoplight (no judgment—I've done it plenty of times!). Go for a walk without listening to music or a podcast. Better yet, leave your phone at home. You can even give yourself a day free of email and social media.

Once you've minimized distractions to the best of your ability (remember, our world is designed to distract, so you can't control all of them!), set an internal intention to be present in your everyday moments. Focus your full attention on the other person when having a conversation. Go for a walk and notice everything around you. Sit in a meeting with your computer closed and participate completely. No need to judge yourself when you wander away from the present moment. Think of it this way—every time you notice you're *not* present, you actually *are* present. The noticing brings you back to the present moment.

How can you minimize distractions so that you can be present and create an environment where joy can thrive? Write down five things in your journal that you can do immediately.

Give yourself permission to be "unproductive"

My client Jessica is a structured, driven person. She had structured her life for productivity. Early morning exercise, set work hours at the office, dinner on the table by six each night. She followed her structure to a T, in an effort to manage stress, and felt like she was breaking a rule if she veered from the schedule.

Ironically, she discovered that following this productive schedule actually *increased* her stress and overwhelm at times. She realized that following the rules she had created for herself got in the way of joy. Some structure was helpful, but she had gone overboard and needed an adjustment.

Jessica started by letting go of the rule that dinner had to be served by six. Instead, she allowed for a twenty-minute family walk with her husband and two little girls after they all got home from work and day care. Yes, dinner was a little later, but the joy was well worth it. She said their entire evening improved because they took the time to slow down and take a walk together.

She also gave herself permission to take time for herself and relax more in the evenings. She told me on one call she had spent an hour one night that week sitting outside reading as the sun went down. I could hear her smiling as she said the words.

In many ways, joy is productive. When you're operating from a place of joy, you will have a bigger impact. Ideas will flow more easily. People will be attracted to your joy and want to work with you.

Often, however, joy requires us to let go of the traditional notion of productivity. Joy needs you to let go of your to-do list and constant driving. It demands that you release the ego of overachieving and hustling and embrace rest. It demands that you not have a productive, outcome-driven reason for doing everything and just do things for fun.

I need to remind myself of this truth regularly. I've never had a problem doing things just for the fun of it, but work is a different story. It's so easy to get caught up in the world's model of success, even when I know that model is not what

I want for my life. I have to give myself permission over and over again to rest and slow down. You probably will as well.

Give yourself permission to be unproductive and do something just for fun for a minute. Or an hour. Or, god forbid, an entire day. Unhook from the rules, release hustle culture, and just *be*.

Play more

A few months ago, my spiritual community did a series on play. It was about returning to your childhood and letting go of the internal barriers that hold us back from being our true selves and regaining the freedom that comes along with play. We called it "Welcome to the treefort."

As part of the series, I got to lead our group in camp songs and games. As a former camp counselor and die-hard camp fan, this was not a stretch for me. I even dressed the part, wearing a glittery puffy-painted shirt and crazy ribbons tied around pigtails in my hair.

We started with a song called "Boogaloo" that involved shouting, stamping your feet, and acting like Frankenstein and a funky chicken. This crowd was pretty accustomed to dancing and singing, but I could tell people were holding back a bit. Joy was creeping in, but the barriers to maximum joy were still alive and well.

After the song, we moved into the gym. I lined everyone up on one side of the room and asked them to run as fast as they could across the gym—while screaming. "This is your chance to release anything holding you back," I challenged them. "Let it all out in that scream!"

And release they did! A switch flipped with that screaming run. Huge smiles appeared on their faces. Bodies loosened up. Enthusiasm rose. They gave themselves permission to be silly and play—and joy came screaming in.

Joy remained as we did a Hula-Hoop relay and played tag. Instead of a bunch of adults, they looked like kids playing. Fifty-year-olds sprinted out of the way to dodge an incoming tagger. They giggled. They huffed and puffed and sweat—and they kept playing. It was an amazing sight.

It can be weird to play as adults. I've felt the internal barriers of really letting down my guard to play. The inner critic comes soaring in with doubt. What will people think if I *really* dance? Am I going to look dumb if I put on a costume and play make-believe—even when I'm with a bunch of kids?

Play is vulnerable. But it's also joyful, creative, and freeing. In true play, there's nothing to prove. It doesn't matter who wins. The overachiever has no role in play. The ego is gone and you're fully in joy.

It's time to bust through the vulnerability and let yourself play. Once you start, it's like breaking a dam—just a trickle at first, as the barrier gets broken down, but soon you have a bursting flow of play. And joy.

My best advice to embrace play is to get around kids. Young kids—those who haven't yet started to feel weird putting their full energy into play. If you have them yourself, this should be pretty easy. If you don't, borrow a few. I have no doubt you have friends or family that would love a free babysitter for two hours.

Once you're with the kids, remove distractions from joy,

set the intention to be present, give yourself full permission to be present (see how all these go together?!) and *play*. Put on a costume. Pretend you're a mermaid. Make up a story. Get on the floor. Belt out a song. Feel the internal pushing and driving slip away as you play, releasing the overachiever and letting in joy.

Notice joy in your everyday life

In chapter six, I shared that we are programmed to remember everything negative. Our brains are wired to be constantly searching for risks and problems to solve—and then remember them as a threat to avoid in the future.

On the other side of the equation, you have to purposefully imprint joy to remember it fully. You need to notice it. Savor it. Feel it in your body. Take it all in. Only then will you remember it in the same way as the negative encounters in your life.

I'm not asking you to ignore risk. Instead, purposefully noticing joy balances things out. In *How Remarkable Women Lead* by Joanna Barsh and Susie Cranston, the authors share that optimism is *more* realistic than pessimism. Noticing joy gives you a more complete and accurate view of the situation and your life as a whole.

This isn't a one-time reflection. It's an everyday practice—a muscle you need to flex regularly for it to strengthen. Practicing the other steps in this chapter will get you into a state of joy. Once you start to feel joy creep in, stop and notice it. Really feel the joy. Let it fill up your entire body. Be present with every last morsel of joy. Notice how it feels in your body and take a snapshot in your mind of the joyful moment. Enjoy it all.

Create your Bliss List

The final piece to reclaiming your joy is to know exactly what brings *you* joy. It's time to make your personal Bliss List of the activities, people, and environments that are most likely to induce joy for you. Combine these with noticing joy in the everyday moments, and you'll be well on your way to reclaiming your personal joy.

- Joyful activities: Does the whole world float away when you paint? Do you always belly laugh to the movie *Dumb and Dumber*? Does watching the sunset fill you with joy? There is no right or wrong here.

- Joyful people: Who are the people in your life who make you feel amazing? These are the people who bring out your joy—and never leave you feeling shameful. Who are your joy people?

- Joyful environments: Are there certain places or environments where you tend to feel greater joy just by being in them? Nature is my most powerful joyful environment. Listening to great music in a small club where everyone is dancing is a close second. What are yours?

Now that you know what they are, start incorporating items on your Bliss List into your life. Every time you experience joy, your true inner voice has come alive. You are awake and living with everything inside of you. You deserve this! You have an innate, divinely given right to a life filled with joy. Embrace that right and create the space for joy in your life.

CHAPTER ELEVEN

redefine success

In ninth grade, I wrote a paper on my definition of success for a class on career exploration. Here is part of my essay:

> *I had to think long and hard about what success is to me. This is especially since I don't have a clue what I'll be doing in twenty years, let alone where or with whom. But I'll tell you what I do know about success. First of all, I think there are many aspects of success and I probably can't achieve them all in a lifetime.*
>
> *Happiness is my number one feeling when success comes to mind. By happiness, I don't mean a happy-go-lucky jumping for joy kind of person. I mean that happiness is an overall feeling of contentment. I think that contentment, or happiness, comes in many different ways and is different for all types of people. . . .*
>
> *Power is another thing that contents me. Not necessarily power over a company or large groups of people, but power over myself. To know that I have the power to control my actions and words. That other people don't control me—I do what I want regardless of what others think of me.*
>
> *Accomplishment is my final contentment. . . . I believe to accomplish the impossible, one must let go of the fear of failure. JFK once said, "Those who risk dismal failure are also those who accomplish great triumphs." There's also a line in the poem "Reaching for*

Rainbows" that says, "If we don't attempt to get over our doubts and fears, we'll never know what it is to live without them." I strongly believe that both of these statements are true and that I must let go of my fears to become successful as a person.

Along with happiness comes living. I want to be able to live my life to the fullest. . . . I want to travel, learn new things, and experience different situations, good and bad. I want to live in the moment, not dwelling on the past or putting pressure on my future. . . .

Now I have a short definition by Bessie Anderson Stanley that basically sums up my feeling on success. "To laugh often and much, to win the respect of intelligent people and the affection of children . . . to leave the world a little better . . . to know even one life has breathed easier because you have lived, that is to have succeeded."

Before we go any further into this, can we stop for a moment and applaud the wisdom of our teenage selves? Yes, we were all full of angst and hormones and undoubtedly drove our parents crazy (I also had a paragraph in this essay on family where I wrote, "My family is very important to me, even though I don't always act like they are"), but I look back at this definition and see how true it is for me even today.

I wrote this at the end of ninth grade—which was also the beginning of my deep dive into overachieving. You can see the natural achiever coming out in me with naming accomplishment as a top definer of success, but also the knowledge that I can't accomplish everything (something

I clearly forgot for many years) and the need to expect and embrace failure to have success (another forgotten lesson). I actively didn't want to put pressure on my future (that didn't work out so well!).

There's also a bit of the "screw it, I'm going to do what I want and see the world and carpe diem every single day, I don't care what you think" attitude that definitely still prevails inside of me today. I love that I acknowledged in the first paragraph that I had no idea what I wanted to do with my life. A desire for happiness came right after that. It's the last paragraph that really gets me, though. I read that quote and it still hits directly at my heart as the truth of my definition of success.

This paper has a completely opposite tone of the poem I shared in the introduction, which I wrote three years after this essay. A poem about how I feared failure so much that I didn't even see it as an option. A poem about disappointing people and worrying they wouldn't be proud of me. A poem written by the voice of an overachiever instead of my true inner voice.

Even though I would have resonated with this fifteen-year-old's definition of success, even when I was in full-force achiever mode, I wasn't living that definition. I knew it to be true in my heart, but I wasn't showing up that way in my day-to-day life. For years, I lived by an outdated and misaligned definition of success—and I'm guessing you have too.

The first part of this book was dedicated to how that definition of success came about in the first place. You learned to define success based on the rules of your parents, school, and our culture as a whole. Proving yourself became a driving force to reach that old way of thinking about success. The rewards you got reinforced that you were thinking about success in the right way, even if it didn't feel completely right to you.

Over the last several chapters, you've done exercises to reconnect to yourself. You've let go of the rules no longer serving you, slowed down, started listening to your body and your true inner voice, rediscovered your creativity and self-expression, and reclaimed joy. Now you get to bring that all together to create a new definition of what success means to you now.

Just like twenty-five years ago, I've thought long and hard about how to define success. And also just like twenty-five years ago, I know that definition will be different for each person. But there are components that will be true for everyone. Here is my equation for success:

Desire x Being x (Impact + Meaning) = Success

Let's pull apart each of these components. They are in no particular order and I believe they are all critical for your truest success in life. The kind of success that feels good in your soul.

Desire

Desire is a sticky word in our culture. It often goes right to sexual desire and has a connotation of lust or greed or something we aren't supposed to want, but do actually want.

Desire can also feel selfish, like it's all about you with no regard to what other people need or want.

Women aren't taught to desire in our culture—and that's exactly why I use this word. There is unbelievable power in claiming your desires. You are standing up and telling the world you're no longer going to play by the rules you've been taught. You are taking up space and forging your authentic path, no matter what anyone else thinks about it.

Desire is also vulnerable (power and vulnerability often go together). When you admit to yourself what you really, truly want in life, you open yourself to the possibility you might not get it. Or you might not get it right, especially the first time you take a step out and act toward your desires. This can be just as hard for a perfectionist as not getting it at all!

No one ever said the path of the true inner voice is easy; however, it's *much* easier than living a life that's not your own. Stating your desires and walking toward them satisfies the soul. This is why desire is part of the equation for success—and why you're going to get clear on your desires right now.

Using these prompts to jump-start your thinking, write down in your journal what you truly desire in your life. Throw away any barriers of what you think you *should* want during this exercise. There is no *should* in desire. Your responses can be related to any aspect of your life—work, relationships, where you live, creativity, travel, the crazy dream you've always had to do stand-up comedy. Everything is on the table!

- What is the secret desire you've always known in your heart, but had a hard time admitting to anyone?

- What would be worth doing even if you know you might fail? (I'm borrowing this question from Brené Brown—it's one of my favorites!)

- What would your ninety-year-old self regret *not* doing in this life?

Being

A few years ago, the former head of the organizational effectiveness department at Cargill (and my former boss's boss's boss), Rae Lesmeister, launched a blog called *Significance Matters*. On the website, she included two separate bios—her human *doing* bio and her human *being* bio. Her human doing bio includes her consulting business, corporate experience, education, and nonprofit board work. Her human being bio says things like: soulful and spiritual, adventurous, challenger, boundary stretcher, and revels in the success of others.

I had never thought about a human *being* bio and I loved it. It's a completely different take on our accomplishments. It doesn't matter what awards you've won or the promotions you've received. It's about who you are at your core.

The overachiever defines success based on the outcome of *doing*. While we need to take action and do in order to have an impact (more on that in the next section), it is just as important to be the person you want to be. Unfortunately, the *doing* nature of the traditional definition of success often gets in the way of *being* our best and most authentic self. Truly, is anyone at their best when they're running around in manic mode feeling the pressure to hold up standards they aren't even sure they really want? *No.*

Your new definition of success must be clear on the person you want to be. Knowing who you are and showing up as that person in your day-to-day life is a big part of a successful life. It's time to bring your full self forward and be visible on the outside as the human you are on the inside.

Just like the section above on desire, use these prompts to brainstorm and clarify what it means to you to be a successful human *being*:

- The most basic and root question of them all—who are you?
- What is on your human being bio?
- How would you want your closest friends to describe you?

Impact + Meaning

This is the closest we get to the overachiever in the new definition of success. The difference is, this kind of achievement is aligned to your values. It is fulfilling and deeply meaningful. It satisfies your soul and has a positive impact on the world, no matter how tiny the impact may be.

Impact and meaning answer the questions, "Why am I here? What is my purpose?" I know those are deep, existential questions, but don't be overwhelmed! I'm not asking you to define your *one* purpose in this lifetime. In fact, I believe the search for a singular purpose can keep you from reaching your fullest potential and making the greatest impact you can with your life.

For years, I felt like success meant having *one* big thing in my life. My *one* passion, *one* mission, *one* true cause that I would be motivated to work on for the rest of my life. For over a decade, I searched for that one thing. In college, I thought it was the environment, so I studied conservation biology. I was passionate about the environment. I sat on street corners in college asking for signatures on a petition to ask petroleum companies to stop their proposal to drill in the Arctic National Wildlife Refuge. I studied tropical ecology in Costa Rica. I taught environmental education and led outdoor trips with teens for the first few years after I graduated.

I still feel strongly about the environment, but the jobs in that field didn't align with my interests, so, after a few years, I left it behind from a work perspective and went back to searching for my *one* thing. I read a book called *The Pathfinder*, which told me that my true passions were in communication and education. From a broad perspective, this is definitely true, but what the heck does that mean in real life? I could do a million things within those fields! I wasn't looking for a million things—I was looking for *one* thing.

I chose to go back to grad school and get my master's degree in human resource development. I figured people spent a good portion of their life at work, and I wanted to be a part of making that time as enjoyable, healthy, and productive as possible. That purpose motivated me, but I still felt like I was searching for my *one* thing.

In my late twenties, I finally realized that I was never going to have one thing. Instead of being disappointed by this knowledge, it freed me from the shackles of defining success by a singular passion and purpose. There was *nothing* singular about my life. I had times in my early twenties when I had W-2s from four different states in the same year. Even once I had "settled" into corporate America, I job-hopped within my organizations like a frog on steroids. I may have been at Cargill for eight years, but I had seven jobs in four locations, including one in Australia, in those eight years. How did I ever think I would be able to choose *one* thing to focus on for the rest of my life?

Now I know that my passions will shift over time. Right now, I define my purpose as a desire to guide women to reconnect with themselves so they can bring their authentic self forward and share their voice in the world. This gives me the energy to get out of bed each morning and get to work. It has motivated me to get out the computer on the days I just didn't feel like writing. Maybe this purpose will keep me motivated for the rest of my life, or maybe I'll have ten more purposes. I don't know—and I'm okay with that.

Beyond shifting career purposes, I realized there are many ways we create impact and find meaning in our lives. The relationships we have with family and friends, volunteering, spiritual communities, creative practices—they all have meaning and create impact.

You know the drill by now. Here are your prompts to clarify how meaning and impact are a part of your new definition of success. Remember, don't overthink it. You already know the answers. Listen to yourself and trust what you hear.

- Where do you derive the most fulfillment in your life? Not happiness—fulfillment. Meaning. Deep satisfaction.

- How do you want people, causes, land, etc. to be different because of you?
- How do you want people to feel after interacting with you?
- What is your work for?
- What impact do you want to have?

Craft a picture of your new definition of success

You've brainstormed your *desires*, the human *being* you are at your core, and what brings *meaning* to your life and how you want to create *impact*. You have all the components of your new definition of success. Now let's bring them together in a single picture—literally.

That's right—you're going to create a vision board! Vision boards are one of my favorite things. I have created them for the last few years in early January, first on my own and now with a group of friends. We even had a check-in last summer where we all provided updates on our visions.

Vision boards are so effective because they provide a visual depiction of what your new definition of success looks like in real life. The process of creating the vision board can also help you clarify your definition, if you had trouble with the brainstorming prompts above.

Before you start, you'll need a poster board, a few old magazines with pictures that you like, scissors, and glue. Feel free to break out art supplies as well. Once you have your supplies, here's what you're going to do:

1. Select a time frame that works for your new vision of success. I recommend one to three years, but it can be longer if you like.

2. Page through the magazines and cut out anything that represents your new definition of success and what that will look like in your life. Both words and photos. Cut out anything that catches your eye. You can decide later what you want to keep.

3. After you have a good stack of clippings, lay them out in front of you. What's missing? Does anything need to be discarded?

4. Once you feel complete, start arranging your clippings. Take another look at your completed vision board before you glue. Does it *feel* like your new definition of success? Does it emanate your desires, the person you want to be, and the impact you seek to create? If so, start gluing! If not, make changes until it feels right. Use markers, paint, stickers, glitter, or any other craft supplies that feel fun to you.

This is a picture of your new definition of success. This updated definition doesn't make you feel behind or manic or like you need to create a massive to-do list and start checking things off. This version of success is aligned and expansive and both calm and exciting at the same time. It is *your* definition and yours alone. Direct from your true inner voice to the page in front of you.

CHAPTER TWELVE

reset boundaries

When I got shingles at age thirty, it was a direct result of *not* doing what this entire chapter is about—setting boundaries.

I went to the doctor quickly when the red spots appeared on my belly, because I'd had an embedded deer tick a month prior and that doctor gave me very strict instructions to return immediately if a rash appeared anywhere on my body. I was pretty sure this unbelievably itchy rash growing down the midline of my stomach wasn't Lyme disease, but I wasn't going to take any chances.

The nurse practitioner looked at my belly. She ran her hands over my skin, feeling the raised swelling. With a question in her voice, she said, "I think this is shingles."

Shingles? I thought. The only person I'd ever known with shingles was my mom, who'd had it while she was going through radiation therapy for cancer treatment. *She* was supposed to get shingles. Ninety-year-olds were supposed to get shingles. An otherwise healthy thirty-year-old who worked out six days a week and ate more vegetables than anyone she knew was *not* supposed to get shingles. There was only one likely cause: stress.

A few months prior to getting shingles, I had accepted an assignment as the project manager for a massive leadership event at my company. Before accepting the additional work, I tried to set boundaries. I asked for a temp to help with administrative tasks. I requested that we cut back on the other programs I was running to focus solely on the event. I was told yes, we'll get you a temp and cut back your other work.

I got the temp. Everything else stayed the same—all the old work, plus the huge new project.

My world immediately shifted into overdrive. I was in manic mode 24/7. I still made time for exercise and occasional fun because that's who I am, but every other second of my day consisted of work. I got to know the evening custodial staff because I was still at my desk when they started working. I often worked late enough at night that I chatted with my colleagues in Europe in real time—it was the next day there and they were already back to work! I was overwhelmed and exhausted when I was diagnosed with shingles and the event was still three months away.

The nurse practitioner gave me a prescription for an antiviral, advised me to slow down, and sent me on my way. That evening I emailed my temp, intern, and two leaders overseeing my work to let them know I had shingles and may be coming in to work late so I could sleep.

I arrived at work the next morning at 8:30 (not exactly late) and got straight to work. At some point during the day, one of the leaders I had emailed came to check in with me and told me to take care of myself. I assured her I would and then turned back to my computer to keep working.

Nothing in my workload changed. My plate continued to overflow, with no end in sight. One day I was so tired I considered crawling under my cube to take a nap. I decided that would probably look a little weird and instead went to the prayer room. I shut the door, settled into the large lounge chair in the middle of the pleasantly dark room, and closed my eyes. A few minutes into my nap, a woman opened the door, someone I assume was actually going to use the room to pray, exclaimed a startled "Sorry!" and shut the door with lightning speed. I was flooded with guilt for taking away her prayer space. Blurry eyed, I got up from the lounge chair, went back to my desk, and never used the prayer room again.

During my entire recovery, no one suggested I take a day off. No one stopped by my desk when they were leaving for the day to tell me I should go home and rest. These were good people who cared about me, but they weren't going to set boundaries for me—and I definitely wasn't setting them for myself.

No one is going to set boundaries for you, either. You've done the work to release old rules, quiet the inner critic, reconnect to yourself, and create your new definition of success. Now you need to *live* it. Boundaries are one of the keys to actually making that happen. You need boundaries to give yourself the space to slow down, let in joy, and hear your true inner voice. Boundaries are the secret to freedom.

Before we jump into how to set stronger boundaries, we need to have a moment of truth about how you're currently spending your time and energy. Take out your calendar. Look over your last two weeks. Now look at the vision board of your new definition of success. Do they align? Does your time and energy match your desires, impact, and the person you want to be?

If you're like most people, much of your work and free time is spent doing things you don't really want to do, but feel like you "should." Yes, I know there are certain things on your calendar that you can't get out of, like the complete-waste-of-time team meeting that happens *every* Tuesday at 8:30 a.m. I also know you have more control and freedom over your time than you think you do. Here's how to set boundaries and spend more time and energy as the real you, living in your new definition of success.

Get to know your yeses

The first step to setting boundaries is to understand what you should be setting boundaries on. If you're accustomed to saying yes to nearly every request that comes your way without thinking, you need to take a step back and decipher the difference between your true inner voice yeses and your inner critic yeses. Here's what each of those different yeses feels like:

Inner critic yes	**True inner voice yes**
• Guilt and obligation	• Alignment to your values
• Feeling like you "should" say yes	• Devotion and commitment
• Desire to feel needed	• Desire to create impact
• You're scared to say no or worried that your no will disappoint someone	• Deep inner knowing that you need to say yes, even though you aren't quite sure why

- Proving you can do it all
- Overwhelm or regret after saying yes
- Contraction in your body

- Curiosity and experimentation
- Joy and excitement after saying yes
- Expansion in your body

We've all experienced an inner critic yes. They are the times you say yes and immediately feel overwhelmed and regret your choice. The day for the commitment approaches and you wonder what you were thinking saying yes. You have no time for this! You wonder if you can back out of it, but you feel too guilty saying no at this point. You go, but are only half-present—the other part of you is daydreaming about taking a nap on the couch because you're completely exhausted from all your yeses.

Sound familiar?

Start paying attention to your yeses. Go back to the exercise on expansion and contraction from chapter eight and use the wisdom of your body to make a decision. An inner critic yes will feel like contraction in your body. A true inner voice yes will be expansive. Let your body tell you the answer. If it's an inner critic yes, then it needs to be a no.

Know what you're saying no to if you say yes

I used to say yes to nearly everything. Not because I felt guilty or obligated, but because I really wanted to do everything! I love to be active, learn, and get involved in new opportunities, but even excited true inner voice yeses lead to burnout, stress, and exhaustion when you pile one on top of another. And another. And another.

I came to this conclusion several years ago when I said yes to a fantastic project at work—heading up mentoring for a brand-new global scholarship and leadership development program for college students around the world. Amazing, right? I thought so, too.

So I said yes without even pausing to think.

I said yes in the same month I returned from a year-long expat assignment in Australia. I had to move back into my condo, rebuild relationships, and learn a whole new job. My new manager advised against me taking on the project, but said it was up to me.

I spent at least four hours a week on this project for the next year. Parts of it *were* amazing. The program was completely aligned to my values. I loved seeing the connections between the students and their mentors. I was completely fulfilled when the students came from Brazil, China, Russia, India, and all over the United States to Minnesota for a leadership seminar, and I got to meet them and hear what they were learning in the program.

I still should have said no.

I realized in the midst of all of this that *when you say yes to something, you're always saying no to something else*. Always. Usually the choices aren't stacked neatly next to each other, so it doesn't look like you're making a trade, but you are.

When I said yes to this amazing project, I said no to leaving the office at a reasonable hour each day. I said no to evenings and weekends free from work. I said no to really enjoying all my social activities because, even though I went out with my friends, my energy wasn't always there to fully engage. I was again overwhelmed, overworked, and exhausted. I didn't get shingles like four years prior, but it was too much.

Once I had this realization, I started to pause before I said yes to new offers. I told people I needed to think about the opportunity and get back to them instead of responding with a yes in the moment. I asked myself, "What am I saying no to if I say yes to this?"

Many years later, I still use this practice. I often still want to be involved in everything. I have to remind myself that the overachiever wants me to do everything, but my true inner voice wants me to focus on the most important yeses in my life. Yeses like this book, which required a massive amount of saying no to find the time to write. When I limit my yeses, I get to dig deeper and contribute more to the few projects I do select, which feeds my soul and creates a bigger impact. Scaling back on yes also gave me more time for rest and creativity and walks outside and lying on the couch watching *The Marvelous Mrs. Maisel.*

The next time your boss asks you to take on a new project or a friend taps you on the shoulder to volunteer for an event, pause before you automatically say yes, no matter how much you want to say yes or how heavy the weight of the guilt riding on your shoulders for potentially saying no. Stop and list what you will be saying no to in your life if you say yes. Time to work on a different project that means more to you? Sleep? An evening at home with nothing scheduled?

Is the yes worth what you're saying no to?

Start saying no more often

It's the obvious next step. If it's an inner critic yes, then you need to say no. If you don't like what you're trading in if you say yes to an opportunity, then you need to say no. When you don't have time and energy for the true inner voice yeses in your life, then you need to say no. It's that simple. And that hard.

Saying no is one of those things you have to just start doing. It will be uncomfortable. Your inner critic will flare up and start convincing you to say yes to avoid the discomfort. Don't be tricked! Be uncomfortable and do it anyway.

While there's no way to make saying no easy when you're not accustomed to setting boundaries, I want to help you get started with a few scripts you can use in your conversations and emails.

- *Due to my other commitments, I must decline.* I love this line and wish I could claim it as my own, but I can't—it's from writer, speaker, and coach Michael Hyatt. It's definitive and leaves no room for asking at a later date (although if you *want* them to ask again later, a simple "for now" at the end will leave that door open). You are clear about your priorities and this new request simply isn't one of them. You get to own it and move on.

- *Thanks for thinking of me, but I need that time to focus on my other commitments.* This is similar to the statement above, but a little gentler. You get to acknowledge your appreciation—and then say no.

- *I'm not going to be able to complete this project and my other work. Let's talk about what's going to come off my plate if*

I do this. This one is perfect for work. When you make this statement, you're showing commitment and healthy boundaries at the same time. You can discuss the drawbacks of doing the extra work in a way that shows the negative impacts to the organization, the bottom line, or your manager. Yes, I realize the answer from your supervisor may sometimes be, "No, I'm sorry—you need to do it all," but I think you'll be amazed at the power of a direct conversation.

- *I'm not able to do that for you right now, but here are some resources . . .* This is another good one for work. You are essentially saying no and helping the person at the same time. You can point them to another person who can assist or to a resource that will help them find the answer for themselves.

- *No.* That's it. Just no. So often we think we need to give a rationale for saying no, but we don't. Think about the last time you said no to a friend who asked you to do something for fun. Did you just say no? Or did your conversation sound more like, "Thanks! That sounds fun, but my manager piled on another deadline yesterday and Jack is recovering from being sick and there's a meeting at church that I really should go to, so I just can't."

You get to decide how much rationale you want to give someone for saying no, but also realize you don't need to give a rationale at all. My friend Alix is *amazing* at this. It was strange for me at first when she declined an invitation without telling me why, but I got used to it. Now I actually admire it. As her friend, I know that she'll be there for me when I need it, and I can also respect that she doesn't owe me an explanation for saying no. She just gets to say it—and you can too.

Start practicing saying these *no* statements. Go ahead and revamp them to sound more natural for you. Create email templates so you don't even have to think about how you're going to say no—you can just copy and paste it. Then embrace the awkwardness of telling someone no and say the words.

Some people won't like your boundaries—and that's okay

No matter how respectfully you decline an invitation or delegate work, some people aren't going to like hearing a no. This is especially true if they have been getting a yes from you for your entire relationship!

I love the movie *Something Borrowed* starring Ginnifer Goodwin and Kate Hudson, who play best friends Rachel and Darcy. While the main plotline of the movie involves a love triangle with Darcy's fiancé, who Rachel has had a crush on for years, what I'm interested in here is the relationship between Rachel and Darcy. Rachel has *zero* boundaries when it comes to Darcy. She complies with every request that comes out of Darcy's mouth, no matter how ridiculous. Finally, about three-quarters of the way through the movie, Darcy makes yet another unbelievable request and Rachel realizes she can't keep saying yes to Darcy for the rest of her life. Rachel gets a little flummoxed trying to confront her over the phone, but then she says a clear, "Darcy, *no*," and hangs up.

Darcy looks like she doesn't know what hit her! She pulls the phone away from her ear and stares at it with total confusion, irritation, and a few choice words!

People might look at you the same way when you start to set boundaries. That's okay. If they're a good friend or trusted colleague, tell them you're working on setting better boundaries. My client Jessica had become the go-to person in her office for extra projects because she was good at what she did and she always said yes. Jessica told her manager she was working on saying no so she could focus on high-impact work, but it was hard for her. She asked him to be conscientious when making an extra request of her. Jessica also got really good at suggesting other people in the office who would be good at doing the extra work. She knew not everyone would like her saying no and delegating, but it was worth it for her to take her life back.

In other words, her no was worth the yes she got in return.

Take action on your boundaries

It's time for you to get specific and take action. Get out your vision board and your calendar again. What's on your calendar that doesn't align to your new definition of success? What inner critic yeses do you need to say no to? List them in your journal. Right now.

Choose one and take action. Pick up the phone and tell the person you need to say no. Send an email declining an invitation. Talk to your boss about the extra project that just got added to your responsibilities. Use one of the scripts in this chapter and make the words come out of your mouth.

It's going to be uncomfortable. All the fears and limiting beliefs you identified in the first part of this book may come roaring back to life (more on this in the next chapter!). Do it anyway. The discomfort you feel is growth toward the life and impact you desire. Freedom is on the other side.

CHAPTER THIRTEEN

reform your fear

You already know that I left my corporate job to start my own business after my true inner voice told me I was lying and my job changed to something I had zero interest in. What you don't know is everything that happened between the realization that something had to change and me actually leaving my job.

The surface answer is that I spoke to a lot of entrepreneurs, I did all the activities in the book *Designing Your Life* by Bill Burnett and Dave Evans, made a conscious decision to start a business, and then walked into my boss's office and gave my notice.

What you couldn't see was the emotional roller coaster happening behind the scenes. On one hand, I was so excited to start my own business! The possibilities felt endless. Ideas flowed out of me. The whole world was my oyster.

And I was also completely terrified.

Starting a business meant quitting my job. It meant telling my parents I was leaving a safe, well-paying career to try something with no guarantees. It meant giving up my health benefits and 401(k) match and great colleagues.

And what if I failed? What if my success was because of the companies I worked for, not me? What if I couldn't hack it on my own and I had to come crawling back to a corporate job?

Ninety percent of the time, excitement and possibilities

won. The other ten percent of the time, I felt like someone had wrapped a corset around my lungs and pulled the strings tight.

The fear was worst in the month before I handed in my resignation. After all, I hadn't actually quit. I hadn't even told my parents. Only a few friends knew my plans. I could still change my mind.

But, in my heart, I knew I couldn't change my mind. Even though I was still doing my job, I was already on a different path. There was no going back once I started listening to my true inner voice. I was moving ahead and fear was just going to be part of the journey.

Fear will likely be part of the journey for you as well. You're letting go of the rules you've been taught and living by a new definition of success. You're setting new boundaries to create space in your life to be your true self. No matter how deeply you need to release the overachiever, it's still scary to let go—even when you're letting go to become the person you really are.

You don't have to quit your job or make a massive life change for fear to come on full force. Simple things like saying no to a commitment you've always accepted can bring out the inner critic in a huge way. Deciding not to work on Sunday evening and walking into the office Monday morning unsure of what's sitting in your inbox can induce a panic attack when you're not used to it.

When we get to the heart of it, I see two core fears appear over and over again when you let go of the overachiever and start living life by your own accord.

1. Failure
2. Disconnection

Let's explore these fears through the lens of a couple women I know.

Katherine's story

Katherine had been a workhorse since middle school. She told me in one of our first coaching calls, "I'm not the smartest person in the room, but I can outwork anyone." That attitude led the way for everything from high school math to her corporate marketing jobs. Katherine worked nights and weekends to get through any obstacle standing in front of her.

There are some real strengths in this attitude. Katherine had grit. She didn't shy away from challenges. She had a huge amount of persistence.

She also believed she *had* to be the workhorse to be successful. She believed her achievement was dependent on the quantity of work she could get through. Katherine's ability to execute massive amounts of work at a high-quality level had brought her to this successful point in her career. All the evidence in her life had proven the workhorse belief to be true.

When Katherine took her first real leadership position, it quickly became obvious this approach wasn't going to work anymore. For the first time in her life, Katherine's job was bigger than she was. Achievement meant influencing and building relationships and getting work done through others. She simply couldn't do all the work herself.

Letting go of the limiting beliefs of her overachiever and listening to her true inner voice wasn't about Katherine quitting her job or moving to the other side of the country. To anyone looking in from the outside, it wouldn't have appeared like Katherine was making any big changes at all. The bulk of Katherine's evolution was internal. Katherine had to let go of her identity as a workhorse. She had to shift her definition of what success looked like in a leadership role and in her life as a whole. She needed to believe the *quality* of her work was more important than the *quantity* of her work.

To move in the direction of these beliefs, Katherine committed to not responding to email during meetings and working only one evening a week. She backed off spending hours upon hours prepping for meetings. She gave herself time to sit and think in the evenings.

It was deeply uncomfortable for her. Fears and emotions came up out of nowhere. She rationally knew it was good to set boundaries, but her old belief system pressured her to speed up and work harder. Her inner critic told her she'd better start acting like the workhorse again before something bad happened.

Over time, Katherine changed her story. I'll never forget the day when she got on our coaching call and told me she was actually starting to believe some of the things we'd been talking about. "I've been doing the things," she said, "but they've been forced. They didn't feel real. Now I'm starting to feel like they could actually be possible."

Over time, others *did* notice changes. Katherine showed up with more authority in meetings with senior leaders. She delegated to her team and empowered them to execute great work instead of taking it on herself. Letting go and slowing down internally allowed Katherine to do her best work externally, even though it was painful at the beginning.

Katherine kept taking action through the fear. She allowed herself to be vulnerable and feel the feelings that came up when she slowed down, no matter how uncomfortable they were. She lived her life with a new definition of success until she truly believed that new definition.

Lindsey's story

Lindsey isn't a coaching client, but I emailed her for input on this chapter because I knew she had been dealing with fear and discomfort as she set boundaries and worked less. Her response was so articulate and beautiful that I wanted to share it with you directly.

> *For much of my career, I ran pretty hard, but I always had the feeling I was only doing enough to keep balls from not falling all around me. It was extremely stressful, it quickly became a habit, and I never felt like I was making an impact in anything I did. To top it off, I felt like I was poorly serving my clients, my staff, and my colleagues.*
>
> *This was also how everyone around me operated. "Busy" was the word that equated to success. However, there came a time when that lifestyle consumed me and, no matter how hard I tried, I*

always felt like I wasn't successful enough and I still needed to do even more.

Part of me transitioning away from my old job was really finding myself. I did that before, during, and after my transition to my new company. However, I quickly found myself on the same train to nowhere, and I knew I needed to get off of it before it crashed. If only I could do that, I would be so much happier and much more calm and centered, right? Well, not exactly. As I spent time focusing on my values and realigning my career drive with my values, I found the time, space, and freedom I was looking for, yet I was still not at peace. As I focused on what was right for me, the world around me kept running at the pace I was originally at. And boy, were those people successful (because that is what success looks like, right? Running a million miles a minute, barely hanging on for dear life). And here I am—spending my time on what is important to me, putting in quality time at work, not working a ton of hours accomplishing nothing, but rather working productive hours making lots of progress, and spending more time back in my community.

At first this felt odd, and lazy. I had a hard time overcoming the mental side of the transition and the belief that if you are busy you are successful and if you are not busy, you are not successful. I had to spend a lot of time overcoming the mental hurdles that I never expected to encounter. I still struggle mentally and I have to work very hard at keeping myself centered on what I define as success and measuring to that yardstick versus some arbitrary yardstick that may or may not be appropriate for me. For me there was a "keeping up with the Joneses" mentality, not from a monetary perspective, but a career self-worth perspective.

I have more challenging days than not right now, but the more I stick with what I know is right, I know that, in time, I will start to really come into the change I desire, which will ultimately allow me to live the life I desire.

Lindsey is *in it* right now. She's in the messy middle. The part of change where you've let go of the old way of living, but you're not yet fluent in the new way. You're taking steps based on faith, believing those steps are leading you in the right direction.

Lindsey also points out all the messages she continued to receive that pointed toward her old definition of success. You have changed. The world has not. Hustle culture still prevails. There will be pressure to conform.

I identify with both Katherine and Lindsey. I've said many times I wasn't the smartest person in my high school class—I just worked the hardest. I worked twice as hard as some of my friends to get the same grades in calculus. Not surprisingly, I kept it up in college, studying *way* more than necessary. I probably could have studied half the amount and gotten the same grades, but my identity was so wrapped up in working hard that I didn't know how to study the right amount.

Fear of failure was part of the driving force for all three of us working so hard, even if we weren't conscious of it at the time. Studying and staying late at the office and checking email on Sunday morning numbed that fear. Overworking shoved the fear down deep, causing consistent underlying anxiety that became a new normal.

It only makes sense fear rises when you slow down. The numbing mechanism—overworking—is gone. You have no barrier to feeling the fear. It's right there staring you in the face, taunting you. It's so uncomfortable that many of us go right back to the busyness.

Fear of failure can also show up when you reconnect with yourself and realize you need to follow a different path in life, like when I left my corporate job to start my business. Even though I had started listening to my true inner voice, I still held tight to the overachiever. I felt like I had to prove myself with nonsensical standards, like matching my corporate salary in a year (which did *not* happen, by the way), and I drove hard to be successful fast. It wasn't until I dove deep into my limiting beliefs and started writing this book that I really began to let go. It's a lesson I've had to learn over and over (more on that in the next chapter).

That's how fear of failure shows up. What about our other root fear—disconnection? I like to call this the "What will they think?" fear. Sometimes it's a very specific "they," like your parents, best friend, husband, or manager. Sometimes it's an ambiguous "they" that doesn't have an actual face or name, but a conglomerate of worrying about what the whole world will think if you do this crazy thing, share this crazy thought, or wear this crazy dress.

I hear this fear from nearly every one of my coaching clients who are trying something new in their lives.

- What will they think if I quit my stable job and start a business?
- What will they think if I wear the shiny red dress?
- What will they think if I say I don't want that promotion?
- What will they think if I say no?
- What will they think if I post that vulnerable thing and show my real opinion?
- What will they think if I wear the bikini?
- What will they think if I tell them I don't want to grow my business this year?
- What will they think if I say I want a million-dollar business?
- What will they think if I share my secret dream?

The list could go on forever. Behind this fear of "What will they think?" is really a deeper fear of not belonging. Instead of "What will they think?" it's more of "What if I do this thing and people laugh? What if I show my true self and they don't want to be my friend anymore? What if I stop achieving in the way people think I should and they don't love me anymore?"

Some of these statements might sound ridiculous reading them, but they are real and legitimate fears underlying much of our behavior. It makes sense that we fear disconnection. Our survival as humans, and especially as women, has depended on being part of a group. Belonging has meant protection; so, when we step out from the crowd and follow our authentic path, fear shows up. This is true for everyone, and when you layer a heightened fear of failure on top of that, it's a double whammy for the overachiever looking to let go.

What to do about fear

The number one rule to managing fear is to remember it's not about making the fear go away entirely. It's about learning to walk forward with the fear. It's recognizing when the inner critic is showing up and saying to it, "Thank you, overachiever, but I need you to back off. You don't get a vote today. I'm going to let you go and do this anyway."

One of my favorite ways to get through fear is to know what is bigger than the fear. When you're clear on what's more important than fear, you allow yourself to be *pulled* through it, instead of *pushing* yourself kicking and screaming through fear and discomfort. Your mission and purpose grow larger while your fear stays the same size, making it easier to move forward.

Take a moment right now to ask yourself: What is more important than the fear of letting go of the overachiever? What's more important than potential criticism or even failure? What purpose or mission is bigger than discomfort?

There are no right or wrong answers to these questions. For some, what's bigger might be spending more time with your family or getting healthy so you can feel good in your body. It may be a cause you're passionate about impacting. On a very deep level, what's most important may be living a life true to yourself, abiding by your own rules, and following your own definition of success.

Whatever it is for you, write down what is bigger than your fear in your journal.

Write a letter to your fear

The next tool for dealing with fear is a fun one—write a letter to it. When I was in the middle of my internal roller coaster before launching my business, I remembered reading a letter Elizabeth Gilbert had written to her fear in *Big Magic,* and I decided to do something similar—write a letter to myself about my fear. Here it is:

> *Heather—you are becoming the person that you want to be. Stepping fully into yourself. Expressing what you have to offer to the world. You are taking the time to design life on your own terms and release the expectations you have created for yourself or others have impressed upon you over many years. Heather, you are creativity, and when you reach into that creativity and act from your heart without ego, your light is unstoppable.*
>
> *And, Heather, you know that stepping into the light can be scary. Light exposes flaws, makes it harder to hide when things go poorly, all eyes on you. But remember when this fear washes over you and you feel vulnerable to the eyes of the world—a life in the light is also warm. It is open, illuminating, and free. It embraces your*

beauty and also your imperfections, knowing that's what makes you real. You've known for a long time that perfection is unattainable—it's now time to act on that knowledge.

But the most important thing to remember, Heather, is that a life in the light isn't about you at all. It is the light you give to others that matters. And only by stepping into the light and bathing yourself in its radiance do you have light to give to others. Overflowing radiance. What might be possible with overflowing radiance?

So when the fear creeps in and sucks the breath from your lungs and the energy from your heart, take a deep breath and turn toward the light, toward the possibilities, inward to your creativity and outward in overflowing radiance.

This letter is essentially a four-paragraph answer to what is more important than my fear. I've read this letter countless times since I wrote it more than two years ago. Whenever I feel the fear edge in, this letter gives me the pep talk I need to keep moving forward, whether by listening to my true inner voice to take a bold action or by slowing down and letting go of the proving overachiever.

I want you to do the same. Write yourself a letter about your fear. Use some of your answers about what is bigger than your fear if you like. Remind yourself why it's important to let go and be your true self in the first place. Tell yourself that you're enough, just as you are. Prompt yourself to remember you are radiant and glorious and fear doesn't take that away.

If you only take one action from this chapter, let it be this:

embrace fear. So often people return to their former ways of being the minute fear shows up because they thought it would be all pink roses and sparkling joy. Expect that fear will show up. Welcome it with open arms. Accept fear and discomfort and doubt and questioning because these are all signs you are growing. You are letting go to become the person you are, your true inner voice alive in the world.

CHAPTER FOURTEEN

the journey continues

Part of me would like to tell you that I've become an entirely evolved, woke being who never cares about the traditional definition of success and has completely let go of the over-achiever.

But that would be a lie.

I've had to learn the lessons in this book many times over. The journey started decades ago when I collapsed on the floor of my parents' kitchen, crying because I was so exhausted. It was the first realization that I actually couldn't do it all. I didn't act on that realization, but it was there.

It continued through my senior year in college when, for the first time, I purposefully studied less. Significantly less. And I got the exact same grades as the semester I stressed myself out so much that I nearly passed out during one of my finals. I started to see I didn't have to work so hard to have an impact. I began unraveling the belief that I had to drive myself into the ground in order to be successful.

I learned the lesson again in my corporate career when I simply stopped working most evenings. I treated it playfully, like an experiment to see what would happen. The answer: *nothing happened.* All the things I felt piling up on me got done the next day.

Then I had to learn the lesson all over again when I started my business. Suddenly success was dependent on me and me alone, so I better push and push and push to prove to everyone (including myself) that I could do it. Because that's who I am, right? I'm not the smartest person in the room, but I can work harder than anyone.

Just now the lesson is sinking into my soul and becoming a part of who I am. I have a new belief now—that I am worthy for who I am, not what I do. I believe that working less will create higher impact while allowing me to be happier and healthier. I don't have to outwork everyone. I don't have anything to prove. I can live by my own rules for life.

The overachiever doesn't own me anymore, but it definitely shows up. Sometimes I even appreciate it. There are aspects of the overachiever that I like and don't want to let go of. I love seeing the impact of my work. I'm not afraid to take on big challenges. I dream big and go after what I desire.

When the negative aspects of the overachiever show up, I catch myself sooner and reconnect back to who I am and what's most important. The overworking spiral shows up less frequently, and I'm able to recognize it and change course faster.

This is real change. It's not a perfect linear line. It's a bunch of squiggles on a page. But, when you look closely, you see the squiggles are moving forward. Inching closer and closer to your truest self, unburdened from the expectations of the overachiever.

Every day our culture will tell you to play by a traditional set of rules. You will see the people around you overworking and tying their worth to external success. You will be pressured internally and externally to buy into that system. It will motivate the overachiever to show up and make an appearance. It's time to create a plan for what you're going to do when that happens. This plan will keep you moving forward on your journey, no matter how messy the squiggles on the page are.

Identify your hot zone

My client Katherine used this term and I love it! Your hot zone is the ramp back up to overachiever mode. It's the signs and signals you're starting to disconnect from yourself and your personal definition of success. It's feeling the old rules creep back in, even though you know they don't actually serve you or anyone else. It's the warning signal that it's time to stop, assess, and reconnect.

The hot zone is going to look different for everyone. Part one of your plan is knowing how you experience it. Here are common signals you're moving into the overachiever hot zone:

- Finding yourself rushing and operating in manic mode
- Working nights and weekends
- Feeling like you have to prove yourself
- Racing thoughts
- Diminished joy from your work
- Saying yes to things you had started to say no to

- Feeling resentment or regret about your commitments
- Underlying current of anxiety or a consistent low-level nervous feeling in the pit of your stomach
- Not giving yourself permission to rest
- Feeling like you're losing control of your workload and/or personal activities
- Numbing activities, like watching endless bad TV or frequent mindless scrolling on your phone
- Craving quiet and stillness on a deep level

My hot zone includes some of these more common warning signs, like the whirring hamster wheel in my chest that happens when I'm in manic mode, and a lack of motivation and joy for the work that typically gives me great satisfaction and fulfillment. My most telltale signs that I'm wandering into the hot zone, however, are jealousy and comparison. I look at other people that I perceive as further ahead than me in their business and I feel behind. The overachiever jumps right back into place and manic mode quickly follows, telling me I better work harder to catch up and fight my way to a bigger business and higher impact.

What are your signs you're moving into the overachiever hot zone? Are there any particular triggers (people, situations, podcasts) that catapult you into the hot zone fast? Write them down in your journal.

Create an if/then plan

You've taken the first step in creating your plan—raising your self-awareness and knowing the triggers that lead you to the hot zone. Now you need a few actions (which, ironically, often involve taking less action!) you can implement to get you out of the hot zone and reconnected back to yourself.

If/then planning is your cure. Psychologist Peter Gollwitzer found that if people created personalized if/then scenarios related to their goals, they were significantly more likely to achieve them. Here's how it works with the overachiever: Your "if" statement is the hot zone warning you listed above. Your "then" statement is the thing you're going to do to reconnect to yourself when you recognize the warning. This book is full of possible "then" actions you can take. For example:

- If I feel the manic mode hamster wheel in my chest, then I will stop and breathe.
- If I feel jealousy and comparison coming on, then I will look at the vision board of my version of success and journal about how I am already fulfilling that vision.
- If I find myself working nights, then I will recalibrate what I need to delegate or say no to.
- If I start scrolling mindlessly through Instagram, then I will delete the app. (Don't worry—you can download it again tomorrow in about thirty seconds!)

- If I am unmotivated and finding less joy in my work, then I will sleep.

Sleep is the most underrated cure and it works magic for me. Often all I need is a nap or a good night's sleep and I'm out of the hot zone without having to do anything else. Hiking or skiing in the woods, journaling, and my spiritual community all bring me back to myself effectively as well.

You can also use if/then statements preventatively for practices that keep you aligned to your boundaries and out of the hot zone altogether. If it's Monday morning, then I'm going to yoga. If I'm asked for my time, then I will pause and ask myself what I'm saying no to if I say yes to that request. If I feel fear coming on, then I will read the letter I wrote to my fear to remind me why I've changed the way I'm living.

What are your if/then statements? Write them in your journal.

Let go of judgment and recognize your progress

The final step in your action plan is the most important: stop judging when you find yourself in the hot zone. Let yourself be imperfect at letting go of perfectionism (because is there anything more ironic than being a perfectionist at working on *not* being a perfectionist?). Forgive yourself again and again when it feels like you're regressing into a person you don't want to be.

You've been operating in overachiever mode for most of your life. It's not going to automatically disappear forever from reading this book, even if you diligently completed every single exercise. It takes time to change your core beliefs about success, failure, and your worth. It requires practice for your body to remember what it's like to move at a normal pace. You need space to adjust to being reconnected to your true inner voice and living by that guiding star instead of the inner critic.

On top of that, remember, the whole world is designed for your overachiever to thrive. Every day, you consciously and unconsciously see messages to push harder and harder and never slow down. It might be as innocent as your colleague's coffee cup that reads, "Coffee. Hustle. Repeat." It could be an upset friend who doesn't understand why you're suddenly declining some of her invitations. It may be the promotion notices you get every time you log into LinkedIn. There is no shortage of pressure for you to keep the pedal to the metal at all times. You'd have to be superhuman to ignore all of it. Give yourself some grace.

When you feel self-judgment coming on and the inner critic popping up in a new way—telling you that you should have figured it out by now, and asking why are you back in the same place you were before and can't you just be done with the process already—instead look for the evidence of your progress. Write down all the ways you've evolved. Make a list of the decisions you've made that honor your true inner voice. The fact that you even noticed you were in the hot zone and are now judging yourself for it is progress. Before reading this book, you wouldn't have even known about the hot zone.

You've come so far. And you were also enough before you

ever started this journey. You get to be both whole and constantly forming at the same time. You are developing and learning every single day, and you are already amazing. You deserve to feel good on the journey. Because it's all a journey.

Redesign your rules for life again and again

We started this book talking about the unwritten rules of your life. These were the rules of your family and culture and your younger self. They were the policies and practices of the overachiever and the woman who had something to prove. Throughout the chapters, you've learned to let go of these rules, reconnect with who you really are, and redefine success according to what it means to you, right now, at this point in your life.

The beauty about creating your own rules for life is that you can re-create them whenever you choose. The definition of success you've written for yourself now may be different in ten years. You'll find new things that bring meaning to your life. You'll discover new outlets for your creativity. You'll encounter people and places and activities that bring you incredible joy and replace half the items on your current bliss list.

You are now on a different path and you don't know where it will lead. Life will surprise you in beautiful ways when you start living aligned to your true inner voice. Your life may change substantially as you listen more and more to that inner voice. You may feel a driving desire to pursue a different career or take up a creative practice you'd never considered. You may find yourself with a strange pull to walk the Camino de Santiago or take your kids out of school and travel for year.

Or not. Your life may not appear to change much at all. But even if your *outer* life doesn't appear to be any different, your *inner* life will be. That is inevitable—and that is what counts. By reading this book, you have already reconnected with a part of yourself. You haven't become a different person. You've become more of yourself.

As you continue to move forward on your path, you will pick up new things along the way that will make you even more of yourself. There will be new lessons, beliefs, people, passions, and curiosities. New ways of being and seeing and journeying through life. The world will change and you will change as a reaction to it. You will endlessly add to the person you are becoming.

You will also continually *shed* lessons, beliefs, people, passions, and curiosities as you walk into your future. You will release expectations and let go of rules that no longer apply to you again and again.

You have the choice to make up new rules to the game at any time. You are never beholden to rules that others set for you or that you set for yourself earlier in your life. The game of life is made up. It's written entirely by you. Create the rules that bring you joy and allow you to contribute at the highest level. Evolve the rules as you evolve.

Knowing yourself is a process that never ends. Reconnect to yourself over and over. Listen to the twinge of your true inner voice. Believe in the possibility that lies within you. Let the whisper of your heart guide your rules for life.

final word

This book is about *you*. It's a journey inside yourself to let go and reconnect to who you really are. I want that for every person reading this book, but it's not my sole purpose for writing. The bigger mission of this book is a desire for you to make a difference in the world. I believe letting go of the overachiever and reconnecting to yourself will make that happen.

When you are guided by a core sense of self, you create your own rules for life. You are no longer tethered to the overachiever or others' expectations or a definition of success that doesn't align with who you really are. You get to speak your true inner voice as your outer voice to the world. You can break barriers and be a revolutionary just by living your life.

The world needs your voice. Not the cookie cutter voice of the overachiever. Not the hustle puppet. Not the imposter voice. *Your* voice. Your truth. This is how you will make a difference in the world.

I'm not saying this to put pressure on you. The beautiful thing about living your truth is that you don't have to *try* to make an impact. It will come naturally. You'll be more creative. You'll listen better to differing perspectives. You'll share a dissenting point of view with your boss. You'll put the idea out there that you've been pondering for months. You'll write the song or poem or book and share it with the world. You'll decide your heart is calling you to start a business or run a nonprofit or become a teacher and you'll go do that thing.

What's more, living by your truth will give others permission to do the same. Standing up and saying you will no longer abide by the rules you've been taught is powerful. Being clear about your desires and sharing them without embarrassment tells other women they can have desires, too. Saying no and setting boundaries with the people in your life gives them direction on how to do the same.

You are about to create a rippling revolution of powerful women ready to take on the world, one unhurried step at a time.

That's why I wrote this book.

acknowledgments

It has been a dream of mine since I was a child to publish a book. As with all dreams coming true, I didn't do this alone. I have so many people to thank for making this possible.

First, to my clients who entrusted me as their coach and allowed me to publish their stories in this book. You motivate me every day to continue working in this field. I am constantly in awe of your courage to do the hard work and make change happen in your lives, workplaces, and beyond.

To all the people who've supported me as I've gone from a corporate employee to business owner and author. My former colleagues who've hired me as a coach or speaker or recommended me for opportunities. The friends who've gotten excited with me as I've launched new projects and programs and who've supported me when things didn't go as planned. My BWC circle of women entrepreneurs who listened to monthly updates on this book for a year and a half and inspired me to keep going. My family and especially my parents, for their lifetime of encouragement.

To all my former bosses who have continually challenged me to grow and cared about me as a person, whether I am working for them or not, including (but not limited to!) Sue Lennartson, Ipek Kursat, Sarah Blomquist, Sue Harrison, Laura Masica, and Shawna Stoltenberg.

To my trio of mentors who I don't actually know but inspire me every day by how they show up in the world: Maya Angelou, Brené Brown, and Elizabeth Gilbert.

To Dara Beevas and the entire staff at Wise Ink for not only shepherding me through this entire process but also consistently reminding me that this book isn't the goal—it's just part of my bigger mission for more women to share their authentic voices with the world.

And, finally, to you. The one who took a chance and bought this book. You are now part of a revolution of women sharing their voices and changing the world, one unhurried step at a time. Welcome.

about the author

Heather Whelpley is a speaker, coach, and author who guides high achieving women to let go of proving, pleasing, and perfection. Heather has led workshops on imposter syndrome, perfectionism, and creating your own rules for success with thousands of people at Fortune 500 companies like Deloitte, General Mills, and Boston Scientific, as well as nonprofits, universities, and professional development conferences. Her signature coaching program, Beyond Perfect, teaches women to break free from overdoing, people-pleasing, and perfectionism so they can reclaim their life while making a big impact. Prior to owning her business, Heather worked in a wide variety of leadership development and human resources roles at Cargill and Ameriprise for ten years. Heather has extensive global experience, including living and working in Australia and Latin America. She has a master's degree in human resource development from the University of Minnesota and is a graduate of the Coaches Training Institute. *An Overachiever's Guide to Breaking the Rules: How to Let Go of Perfect and Live Your Truth* is her first book.

Read Heather's blog and get all the details about workshops and coaching at www.heatherwhelpley.com

speaking engagements

With over ten years of experience in training and development, Heather knows how to make keynotes and webinars interactive and practical. No death by PowerPoint here! She creates a trusting environment where participants can share their experiences openly. Attendees will be challenged to think in new ways and will walk away with concrete actions to implement.

Heather's core speaking topics include "Imposter Syndrome and What to Do about It," "Overcoming Perfectionism," and "Creating Your Own Rules for Success."

Past event organizers have said:

- "Heather was a smashing hit and elevated our whole conference!"

- "Everyone left Heather's session feeling empowered to define success on their own terms and step into the person they want to be in their career and life as a whole."

- "Heather exemplifies a great blend of expertise, enthusiasm and pragmatism in her facilitation!"

- "Heather knocked it out of the park! Participants told me this was the best topic and presentation this year!"

Contact Heather at hello@whelpleyconsulting.com to discuss your event.

Made in the USA
Coppell, TX
26 October 2021